What a Character!

HEROES OF EARLY AMERICA

Notable Lives from History

Marilyn Boyer

First printing: October 2024

Copyright © 2024 by Marilyn Boyer and Master Books. All rights reserved. No part of this book may be reproduced, copied, broadcast, stored, or shared in any form whatsoever without written permission from the publisher, except in the case of brief quotations in articles and reviews. For information write:

Master Books, P.O. Box 726, Green Forest, AR 72638

Master Books® is a division of the New Leaf Publishing Group, LLC.

ISBN: 978-1-68344-369-8
ISBN: 978-1-61458-884-9 (digital)
Library of Congress Control Number: 2024943363

Cover: Diana Bogardus
Interior: Terry White

Please consider requesting that a copy of this volume be purchased by your local library system.

Printed in the United States of America

Please visit our website for other great titles:
www.masterbooks.com

For information regarding promotional opportunities,
please contact the publicity department at pr@nlpg.com.

Table of Contents

1. Captain John Smith—Adventurer in the New World 5
2. Myles Standish—Protector of the Pilgrims 19
3. Squanto—Friend of the Pilgrims 33
4. William Bradford—Father of the Pilgrims 45
5. Pocahontas—Powhatan Princess 57
6. John Alden—Pillar of Strength 69
7. William Penn—Defender of Religious Freedom 81
8. David Brainerd—Missionary to Native Americans 95
9. Noah Webster—Schoolmaster to America 107
10. Peter Francisco—A One-Man Army 121

Glossary 133

Corresponding Curriculum 139

Endnotes 141

Image Credits

Images are AI-generated at shutterstock.com

Wiki: page 120

Maps: *Map Trek,* page 32

Publisher's note: "Circa" is a Latin word that means *around* or *about*. We use it on certain dates in this book when it is uncertain the exact date on which something happened, but we know it was close to that time.

1

Captain John Smith – Adventurer in the New World

Circa 1580 – June 21, 1631

Who Was Captain John Smith?

John Smith "was a farm boy who grew to be a man who lived a full life of adventure. He conquered enemies, survived storms, suffered injuries, endured slavery, outwitted pirates, defeated rivals, negotiated with American Indians, and played a vital role in the success of Jamestown."[1]

Early Years

John Smith was born in Lincolnshire, England, in 1580. He and his younger brother and sister grew up on a farm his father **leased** from Lord Willoughby. He was privileged to attend the same school as Lord Willoughby's children. John enjoyed exploring the countryside with the Willoughby boys. He did not, however, enjoy school. He was smart, but he had a hard time concentrating. He was dreaming of adventure, and he had a good reason to. He was growing up in a very exciting time in history. Sir Francis Drake had just sailed around the world by ship. John wanted to do something exciting like that, or perhaps be a soldier and become a hero of the battlefield.

leased: Rented

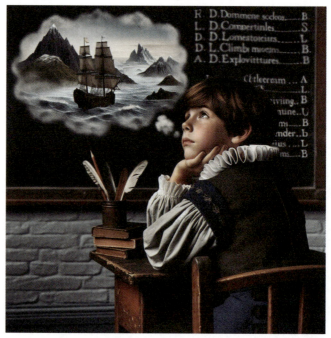

Heroes of Early America

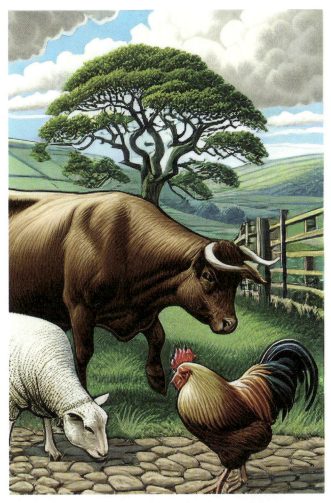

When John was 15 years old, his father **apprenticed** him to a merchant. If he had continued in this trade, he would probably have become wealthy, but it was of no interest to John. He was made to sit and add up endless columns of figures and write endless letters. He was afraid he would be stuck with a life of boredom and unable to create a life of freedom for himself.

Suddenly in the spring of 1596, his brother burst through the door and told him his father had died and his mother needed him. Riding home, though saddened at his father's death, he thought that maybe this would be his chance. He would inherit seven acres of pastureland, three orchards, and most of his father's livestock. Maybe he could sell some of it and make himself a life of freedom.

apprenticed: Sent him to learn a trade from a skilled workman

Captain John Smith — Adventurer in the New World   7

Soldier John

John and his friend Robert, one of the Willoughby boys, went to France to visit Robert's brother Peregrine, who was studying in Orleans. They had many adventures along the way. When the month was over, John could not stand the thought of going home to his unsatisfying apprenticeship. However, he had used up all the money he had brought. He had to find employment somewhere. He joined up with a group of **mercenaries** who were fighting alongside the French army.

Protestant King Henry IV of France was in a struggle against Catholic King Philip II of Spain. They were fighting for the future of France. John discovered that mercenaries received no actual wage but made their money by **looting** the homes of **traitors**. He was given food, a helmet, and a uniform. If he wanted a blanket to stay warm at night, he had to find one after a battle. He arrived after a battle had occurred, went into a stable, and found himself a horse, a saddle, a woolen cloak, and a new sword. However, he soon realized his heart was not in this cause. He decided to move on to another adventure.

mercenaries: Hired professional soldiers

looting: Confiscating goods in a war

traitors: Those who betray their country

Heroes of Early America

Training

John returned to England. He was 19 years old and did not know what he wanted to do with his life. Not long after his return, he met an Italian man who was a famous horseman. He taught John how to ride at top speed and skillfully use his weapon while riding. He told John incredible stories of the Crusades — battles occurring in Eastern Europe against the Turks who were trying to take

over Europe and force their religion on Christians. The Christians were fighting to defend their lands. John thought this was something he could fight for. He read books about warfare. He trained for a year with his Italian friend to learn **strategies** for fighting, horsemanship, and hunting. What he learned during this time would help prepare him for his time in America.

strategies: Plans to achieve military successes

Headed for the Crusades

John boarded a ship to sail to France. He realized that most of the passengers were Catholics. John stood out as an Englishman and therefore, a Protestant. When a fierce storm began, one of the passengers hollered, "All Englishmen are pirates!" That started a riot

Captain John Smith — Adventurer in the New World

and the passengers tossed John overboard. They claimed that the storm was sent because God was angry that John was on board.

John fought the waves, almost drowning, but eventually, he saw an island in the moonlight. He swam toward it and, using all his energy, managed to drag himself to the edge of the shore. He was too exhausted to even pull himself totally out of the water. He lay face down in the sand. When morning came, he slowly arose and walked on the beach for about a mile. There was no sign of life anywhere. Then he spotted a ship and waved wildly to flag it down.

The ship came to pick him up. It was owned by a group of Bretons, residents from Brittany in France. John told his sad story to the captain, and the captain asked him to join his group of **privateers**. John didn't have much choice. He could either join them or be **marooned** on a deserted island. So for the next six months, he sailed all over the Mediterranean seeing places he'd never dreamed of. Along the way, the ship attacked and **plundered** smaller ships. During this time, John learned much about sailing and seamanship.

privateers: Privately owned, armed vessels hired to attack enemy ships

marooned: Stranded

plundered: Took goods as an act of war

When John walked off the ship in Naples, Italy, he had 225 **pounds** in his pocket. He purchased a new **suit of armor** and a horse.

Hero John

At last, he met up with the army of **Archduke Ferdinand**, which was fighting the Turks. John fit right in with the different cultures represented by the soldiers. With his language skills, he could communicate with more of the men than anyone else in the regiment. This brought him to the attention of his commander. This officer asked if John had any ideas about how to relieve a Hungarian town that was under siege by the Turks.

pounds: British money

suit of armor: Protective clothing made of metal

Archduke Ferdinand: Ruler of Austria

It so happened that John had met the commander of the besieged soldiers when he first joined the army. They had spoken about a new method of communicating, using lights and torches. John worked out a plan and hoped the trapped commander would remember their talk. They used a system of fireworks to communicate. The commander responded with lights that indicated that he remembered. John set the plan in motion, which allowed them to attack the Turks from the rear and liberate the town of Oberlimbach. John's commanding officer was so impressed with

Captain John Smith — Adventurer in the New World

John that he promoted him and gave him command of a unit of 250 **cavalry** soldiers.

Now the officer gave John another problem to solve. Alba Regalis was a city that had been held by the Turks for 60 years. Once again, John devised a plan for **liberation**. He filled earthen pots with gunpowder and covered them in pitch and turpentine. Musket balls were placed in the pitch and the unit was covered with canvas. A linseed-soaked wick was placed in each pot. John called these pots his "fiery dragons." **Catapults** were put in place and aimed at Alba Regalis. The attack began at midnight. The wicks were lit, the "dragons" were catapulted into the city, and they exploded, setting fire to the buildings. Musket balls were sent flying in all directions. After 60 years, Alba Regalis was finally free. John was once again known as a hero and his **exploits** became known throughout the Austrian and Hungarian armies.

cavalry: Soldiers on horseback

liberation: Freeing them

catapults: Launchers

exploits: Daring feats

Heroes of Early America

Jousting Victories

In the spring of 1602, John and his troops were getting ready to attack a **fortified** city in Hungary. Before the battle could begin, the lord of the city challenged any English officer to **joust** to the death. John had been well trained by his Italian friend. He accepted the challenge. He knew the **visor** was the weakest part of any armor, so he aimed for the visor and was victorious. The man's friend challenged John to another jousting match first with lances and then pistols. Again, John was the victor. He won a third time as well. The commander of his regiment was impressed with John's performance. He gave him a generous reward, a coat of arms, a portrait of gold, and money. The motto on the coat of arms was, "To Conquer Is to Live." Later, John was engaged in another battle in which his men lost, and he was injured, taken prisoner, and sold as a slave. In a narrow escape, John took off on horseback and was free.

fortified: Protected

joust: Contest with lances

visor: Armor covering the face

Return to England

John returned to England in 1604. He found things very different from when he had left more than three

Captain John Smith — Adventurer in the New World   13

years earlier. Queen Elizabeth I had died and King James had taken the throne. The king wanted to conquer more lands around the world. John met a man named Bartholomew Gosnold. He had been to America and thought it was an **opportune** time for some Englishmen to start a colony. He realized John had many talents and skills that would be valuable and invited him to join his team. Always up for adventure, John agreed.

There was much involved in planning for a trip of over 5,000 miles. First, they had to convince others to brave the difficult journey. Second, they had to raise the funds needed for food and supplies. Supplies were needed for the five-month journey and there had to be enough to last while they were building the new colony. Lastly, they needed to convince King James of the **merit** of such an undertaking. John began learning the native languages he would need to communicate with Native Americans in Virginia. He also studied how to create maps. It took two years of preparations. They were able to convince the "Virginia Company of London" to finance the trip. The Virginia Company was a group of men wanting to invest in the New World. In return, the investors wanted gold or furs.

opportune: Favorable

merit: Advantage

Off for America

Captain Christopher Newport was chosen to command the expedition. He had fought with Sir Francis Drake and was familiar with the area around Virginia. Three ships made the journey. On New Year's Day 1607, all 144 passengers and the Virginia Company of London gathered for prayer. A sermon was preached by Reverend Robert Hunt, who had been selected as the expedition's chaplain. Sealed boxes were given to each captain of the three ships. Upon arrival in Virginia, the boxes were to be opened, revealing the names of men selected to govern the new colony. John was assigned to the *Susan Constant*. The next day, on John's 27th birthday, they set sail for America. The seas were rough, and many were frightfully seasick. The ships were terribly crowded, and conditions were very uncomfortable. John passed the time telling about his many adventures. The crew admired him. The trip lasted four and a half months.

Despite conflicts among the crew, on April 26, 1607, they arrived in Virginia. The settlement was named Jamestown, in honor of King James. When the secret box was opened, it revealed that John Smith was one of the six men chosen to serve on the Governing Council.

Powhatan and Pocahontas

While on an exploration trip, John Smith and his men were captured by a band of 200 Native Americans. The men were all killed, but John fought so bravely that the braves decided to take him to their chief. John pulled a compass from his pocket and showed the leader, Opechancauough. He was fascinated by it. In a few weeks, he was taken to see the head chief of the Powhatan tribe. The chief asked John many questions and John knew enough Algonquian words from his studies to communicate. Then without warning, Chief Powhatan called his braves to him. They came nearer with large clubs and forced John to lie down with his head on a large stone. He closed his eyes, knowing he was about to die.

Surprisingly, he heard a girl's voice pleading with Chief Powhatan. It was Powhatan's 10-year-old daughter Pocahontas. She begged her father to spare John's life. He refused, but suddenly she threw herself down, laying her head on top of John's to protect him. Pocahontas was the chief's favorite daughter. He could not resist her pleas and spared

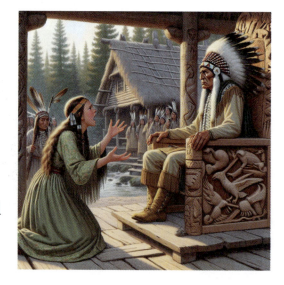

John's life. He turned to his men and said, "There will be no killing today. Pocahontas shall have her way."[2] Chief Powhatan then said, "We are friends now. I will think of you like a son. You may return to your people. I will send men to escort you."[3] John was permitted to return to the settlement. He had been gone nearly a month and the settlers had thought he was dead.

John's Usefulness

John's life was full of more adventures, too many to tell. He led an expedition to the Chesapeake Bay. During the expedition, John was stung by a deadly stingray. He again thought he was going to die, but the doctor used special oils and his arm was healed. He created a map of the Chesapeake Bay area. This map was so accurate it was used for the next 300 years. He was eventually elected President of Jamestown. During his time here he managed through his kindness and strength to win the respect of all the surrounding Native American tribes.

Some of the wealthy settlers **shunned** physical work. So John made a rule, taken from the Bible: "He that will not work shall not eat" (II Thessalonians 3:10). John worked alongside his men. There was no task too **menial** for him to tackle. In a month, they managed to build 20 new houses in the fort, and they dug a well. They also cleared 40 acres of land. John trained the men in the fighting skills he had learned during the Crusades. He established trade with the Native American tribes, which helped supply the colony with food. More settlers came. Chief Powhatan realized that the white men would soon outnumber his people. He knew that John Smith was the reason they were successful. He planned again to kill him. Pocahontas heard of the plot and warned John, once more saving his life.

shunned: Avoided

menial: Lowly

Captain John Smith — Adventurer in the New World

Final Return to England

Unfortunately, John had an accident when a spark from his flintlock gun landed on gunpowder. He was badly burned from his waist to his thighs and was in terrible pain. Of necessity, he gave up his presidency to return to England in order to get medical treatment. On October 4, 1609, John left his beloved Jamestown. He spent the rest of his life trying to return. Things fell apart at Jamestown without his leadership and resourcefulness. The next winter was called "The Starving Time." In eight short months after John left, the fort lay in ruins and 90% of the colonists had died.

While he was recovering, John spent the next several years writing books about his experiences in Virginia. He attempted to return once he was healed, but he was captured by pirates and held prisoner. The pirate ship sank in a storm, and John was able to reach a small island. He was near death when he was found by some hunters. He spent the rest of his days writing books telling of all his many adventures. John never lost his love for America.

Captain John Smith died on June 21, 1631, when he was 51 years old. Although he never made it back to America, he encouraged many others to go there. John's love for adventure, his determination, and his skill in managing others led to Jamestown becoming the first permanent English settlement in the New World.

2

Myles Standish – Protector of the Pilgrims

Circa 1584 – October 3, 1656

Who Was Myles Standish?

Myles Standish was born around 1584 in Lancashire, England. When he was just a small boy, both of his parents died. Not much is known about his early life. Nathaniel Morton, who knew Standish personally, wrote this just after his death: "This year Captain Myles Standish **expired** his mortal life. He was a gentleman, born in Lancashire, and was **heir** apparent unto a great estate of lands and livings, **surreptitiously detained** from him; his great-grandfather being a second or younger brother from the house of Standish."[4] Apparently when Myles was a little boy unable to defend himself, someone cheated him out of land and position that he should have inherited when he came of age. "Myles" is a Latin word meaning "soldier" and that is what Myles became. By his 20th birthday, he was employed as a soldier.

> **expired:** Died
>
> **heir:** Person entitled to inherit property or rank
>
> **surreptitiously:** Secretly
>
> **detained:** Seized

Meeting the Pilgrims

Queen Elizabeth I was ruling England in the late 1500s. She sent English troops to Holland to assist Dutch soldiers in their fight against Spain. Myles was one of the soldiers she sent. While in Holland, he met a group of Christians who were also from England. These people had left England

20   Heroes of Early America

to gain religious freedom. English citizens were only permitted to attend the Church of England. There were important beliefs of that church which the group of Christians did not agree with. They left the country and took their families to Holland so they could worship freely. Their leader was a pastor named John Robinson.

All was well in Holland for a while, but the English **immigrants** soon felt their children were following some bad habits set by the Dutch children. They decided to move again — this time to the New World. In America, they could worship and raise their families freely. As they prepared to leave, they realized they would need men who were skilled in carpentry and other trades needed to establish a community. They had heard reports of Native Americans in the new land and realized they might need someone to help protect them. John Robinson knew Myles Standish. He thought having a soldier along to protect them would be just what they needed. Myles was married but he and his wife, Rose, had no children. They both agreed to join the group that would become known as Pilgrims. Myles was about 36 years old at this time.

immigrants: People who move to another country permanently

Myles Standish — Protector of the Pilgrims

21

The *Mayflower* Trip

Myles soon became a leader, helping to plan for the journey. Even though he was not one of the Pilgrims, they knew they could depend on him to do his job well. On September 6, 1620, the *Mayflower* left England for the New World. On board were 102 passengers. Thirty of that number were the sailors. It was an **arduous** trip. The ship was very crowded. There was no place to take a bath or wash clothes. The ship was not heated. The people ate salt pork or beef, hard biscuits, and dried peas. When the sea grew rough, many people got seasick. It was 66 long days before land was **sighted**. However, they were off course and had landed much farther north than planned. Myles Standish helped them decide to settle where they were since it was already November and the cold of winter was upon them.

arduous: Hard, requiring considerable physical effort

sighted: Seen

The *Mayflower* Compact

Soon after landing, the leaders determined they had to write a document of laws that all must abide by. Myles Standish was one of the first people to sign the agreement. He was **tasked** with exploring the wilderness. He had to be alert to all possible dangers. The Pilgrims needed to build houses before it got too much colder. It was **critical** to find a fresh water supply near the settlement. But Myles Standish's most important job was to see if any Native Americans were nearby and, if so, to establish friendly relations with them.

Myles Standish headed three discovery trips around the new land. Each time he took about 15 men with him. He had started the journey from England as a soldier, but now he was counted as one of their leaders. The Pilgrims had come to trust his judgment. On the first discovery trip, Myles cut firewood for the Pilgrims so they could be warm. They did not locate a water supply at that time. On the second trip, they were still looking for fresh water. Myles and the men carried **muskets** in case they were attacked. This time they saw a few Native Americans who appeared frightened. They ran when they saw the English men. Fortunately, they did find a freshwater spring this time. On the third discovery trip, they saw more Native Americans but did not get to communicate with them.

tasked: Given the job

critical: Important

muskets: Light guns with long barrels

Myles Standish — Protector of the Pilgrims

That night they had to sleep outside instead of returning to the ship, so they built a **barricade** around their temporary camp. They had to take all precautions in case unfriendly Native people attacked. In the morning, the Pilgrims heard strange cries. All of a sudden, arrows started flying at them. Myles immediately went into action.

He had his **flintlock** with him, ready to fire immediately. The Native Americans were frightened by the musket fire and most ran away. One warrior stayed hidden behind a tree and kept shooting his arrows. Myles did not want to kill him, but he did want to stop him. He shot his musket at the tree. The shot splintered the bark of the tree and the man shrieked and ran away.

barricade: Temporary enclosure

flintlock: Gun fired from a spark

Plymouth

Finally, on December 16, 1620, the explorers discovered a quiet, protected harbor. John Smith had called it Plymouth six years earlier. It had plenty of fresh water and an abundance of crabs, mussels, and lobsters. This is where they decided to settle and build their village. It had been six weeks since they first spotted land and at last, they were ready to settle down.

The work went slowly but steadily. Everyone helped. They decided to build 19 cottages and a common house that would be shared by all. Unmarried men lived with families until they could build homes later. Myles was influential in helping to plan the town. Many still slept on the *Mayflower* while construction went on. They carried supplies each day by boat, but they had to walk a mile and a half in shallow water to get to land. Winter had come and the water was icy. People began to get sick.

Construction started on their first building, the common house, on Christmas Day. They knew they were racing against the weather. They had to get shelter or they would all die. The common house went up quickly because everyone helped. However, it soon began to fill up with sick folks. One day in January, the **thatched** roof caught on fire. Many of the sick people were too ill to get up. From a distance, Myles saw what was happening and raced to help. He was one of the very few who was not sick. He hurried to move the barrels of gunpowder stored in the common house. They would explode if the fire got too close. He then moved sick people outside. Next, he and some of the other men **extinguished** the fire. No one was killed, but the building needed repair and the sick were getting worse.

thatched: Made from grasses

extinguished: Put out

Myles Standish — Protector of the Pilgrims　　　　　　　　　　　　25

Myles Standish — Commander

The men decided they must form a small army for protection. Myles was chosen to be commander. Unexpectedly, two Native Americans were seen on the top of the hill. They were motioning for the men to come to them. Myles had been waiting for an opportunity for friendly contact. He and one other man approached them, laying down their muskets as a sign of peace. They could hear many more warriors fleeing in the distance. The two who had **beckoned** them turned and ran away. That made Myles uneasy. The English needed to be prepared in case those braves returned to attack. He decided to get busy building his fort and get the cannons off the *Mayflower* for defense.

> **beckoned:** Gestured to

Fort Hill

The colony had one street which lay at the bottom of a steep hill. The men all agreed that Myles should build his fort at the top of that hill. He could mount his cannons there and have a good view of the surrounding area. They also advised him to build his house at the foot of the hill. Then he would have easy access to the fort if danger arose. They called the location "Fort Hill."

Heroes of Early America

As a result of the icy cold weather, some of the Pilgrims came down with **pneumonia**. Others had **tuberculosis**. Two or three people were dying each day. Myles' wife, Rose, died on January 29, 1621. Myles was kept too busy to grieve. He never did get sick. He would gather wood and keep the fires burning, cook food for the others, feed the weak, and keep them clean. When people died, the job fell to Myles to bury them. He was careful to do this in the dark so Native Americans would not see how many people were dying. By the end of the winter, half the people who had sailed on the *Mayflower* were dead.

pneumonia: A bacterial or viral lung infection

tuberculosis: A serious illness affecting the lungs

Samoset

On March 16, the Pilgrims were surprised when a lone Native American walked into their camp and said in English, "Welcome, Englishmen!" He told them his name was Samoset. Samoset was a leader from the Abenaki tribe located in Maine. He had been visiting Massasoit, the great Wampanoag chief. He had learned some English from trading with English fishermen. That is why Massasoit asked him to go meet the English and try to find out why they were there. The area in which they were living, Samoset said, was called Pawtuxet. He related that most of the tribe who had lived there died in a great plague four years earlier. Samoset ate with the Pilgrims and stayed all night. The next morning, he told them he would return in a few days with some of the **Wampanoag people** so they could begin to trade with them.

He also told them there was another tribe in the area that was not friendly to Englishmen, the Nausets.

Squanto

On March 22, Samoset returned, this time with a brave named Squanto from the Pawtuxet tribe. He had survived the plague only because he had been kidnapped and taken to England. Massasoit, the Wampanoag chief, was on his way with 60 braves. Captain Standish took some men to meet him and **escort** him to the camp. Massasoit agreed to meet with Governor John Carver. A peace treaty was established — the first of its kind in America. Massasoit honored the treaty his entire life. In it, they promised never to attack each other and to come to each other's aid if attacked.

Wampanoag people: Native American tribe living in that area

escort: Lead

28

Heroes of Early America

By summer, only 52 people who came on the *Mayflower* were still alive. Squanto decided to live with the Pilgrims. He acted as a translator and taught them many survival skills. They had a bountiful harvest in the fall due to Squanto's help. They celebrated a feast with their Native American friends. This became known as the First Thanksgiving. Its purpose was to thank God for helping them survive their first year in America.

Hobomok

Another Native American joined the Pilgrims. His name was Hobomok. He became a good friend to Myles Standish. He lived in Myles' house for many years. Myles, being a military captain, not only protected the colonists but explored the area trying to **procure** supplies. He traded with Native Americans for corn and other goods. One day, Hobomok came running to inform Standish that Squanto could be dead. He and Squanto had visited with a chief from another tribe who was angry with them for

procure: Obtain

befriending the English. Hobomock had run off to get help when he saw the chief approaching Squanto with a knife. He did not know what happened to Squanto. Captain Standish flew into action. He took 14 men and set off to help Squanto. They marched into the chief's hut in the dead of night. Only the chief's family was there. Standish promised no one would be

Myles Standish — Protector of the Pilgrims

hurt if they turned over Squanto. The rest of the tribe was frightened by Standish and his band of men. They gladly released Squanto and asked for peace.

Myles Standish protected the Pilgrims many times and tried to establish peace with all neighboring Native American tribes. He directed the Pilgrims to build a fence 11 feet high around their village. It protected their homes and water supply. He also organized the men into groups and appointed commanders to guard sections of the wall if attacked. He drilled and trained the men. He also instructed them on what to do in case of fire. Myles commanded the small army at Plymouth for 30 years.

More Colonists Arrive

More ships arrived from England after several months. More people wanted to join their colony. A woman named Barbara arrived on one of these ships; she became Myles' new wife. Some scholars think she may have been Rose's sister. Myles and Barbara were married and had five children. Myles and his family worshiped with the Pilgrims. Worship services were

held in his fort. In 1624, he became one of the assistant governors and the treasurer of the colony. He held these positions for most of his life. Along with a few other men, he also took on the responsibility of paying back the English government the money it had loaned the Pilgrims for their journey. He established trading posts around Plymouth. It took six years, but he paid off the debt and the Pilgrims were free to keep the money they earned.

Gradually, as more settlers came and Plymouth grew, Myles Standish helped to start a new town. It was called Duxbury, located across the harbor from Plymouth. The Standish family moved to Duxbury and two of Myles' sons held important positions there. One of his sons became a leader in the Duxbury church.

Faithful Myles Standish finally became very sick and died at the age of 70. He had asked to be buried in Duxbury near his daughter who had died before him. Standish's heart was with the Plymouth Colony. "Myles Standish proved to be uniquely suited to ensuring the survival of the colony against incredible odds. Had he not been on the *Mayflower*, Plymouth would likely have failed, and the history of an entire continent, and therefore the world, would look very different."[5]

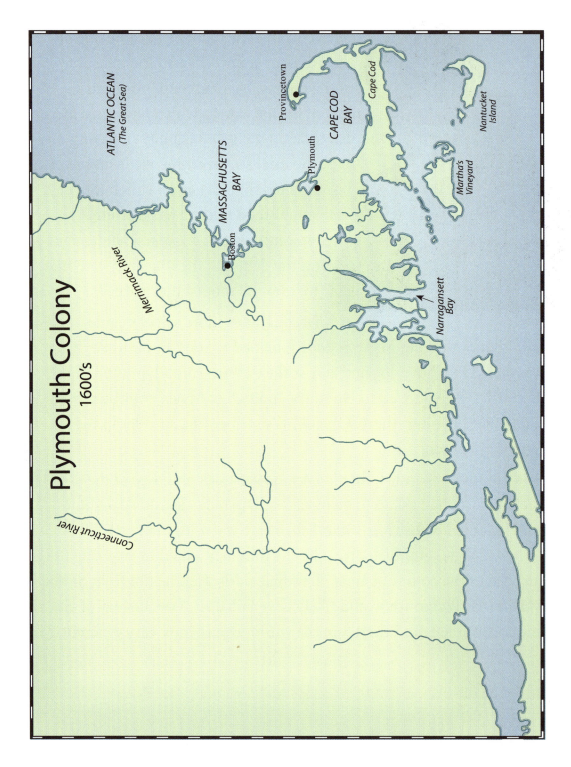

3

Squanto – Friend of the Pilgrims

Circa 1585 – November 30, 1622

Who Was Squanto?

Squanto, a Native American, was a member of the Pawtuxet tribe who lived in what is now Massachusetts. Through a trying set of circumstances, he became a dear friend to the Pilgrims and is credited for helping them survive in the New World.

Early Years

Squanto was born sometime around 1585. The name given to him at birth was Tisquantum, but later, the Pilgrims shortened his name to Squanto.

In 1614, an expedition led by Captain John Smith was sailing along the coasts of Maine and Massachusetts Bay. They were making maps of the area. They also stopped along the way, trading with tribes of Native Americans for furs and fish. When the maps were complete, Smith left for England in one of the ships. He left Thomas Hunt in command of the second ship.

Hunt was to secure the haul of cod fish. He would then deliver it to Malaga, Spain, where there was a good market for dried fish. Unfortunately, Captain Smith did not realize that Thomas Hunt was a greedy and unprincipled man. Hunt decided to sail to Plymouth Harbor to lure some Native American men onto his ship.

His plan was to take them to Spain and sell them there as slaves. He intended to pocket the money for himself. The Pawtuxet tribe agreed to meet with him under the **pretense** of wanting to trade for beaver pelts. He was able to trick 24 Native Americans into coming aboard his ship. Squanto was one of them.

Hunt locked the braves up in the bottom **hold** of the vessel for the entire journey to Spain.

> **pretense:** False appearance

> **hold:** Place for storing cargo

Squanto Is Rescued

Captain John Smith was outraged when he heard what Hunt had done. He later wrote that Hunt had "most dishonestly and inhumanely, for their kind usage of me and all our men, carried them with him to Malaga, and there for a little private gain sold (them) for **rials** of eight."[6] Once in Spain, the captives were marched into the town square. Most of the men were sold in the European slave market. Two kindly **monks** came forward, held up a cross for all to see, and took **custody** of Squanto and the remaining braves. They took them to the **monastery** and for a few weeks, taught them the Christian faith. The monks cared for the men,

> **rials:** Unit of Spanish money

> **monks:** Catholic religious men living under strict rules

> **custody:** Protective care

> **monastery:** A building where monks live

Squanto — Friend of the Pilgrims

who had been weakened from the trip. One by one, they helped them find people who would give them jobs and treat them well.

Off to London

Squanto was taken to London, England. Here he came to live with a rich merchant named John Slaney of Cornhill, London. Mr. Slaney was the treasurer of the Newfoundland Company that had financed the establishment of a colony in Newfoundland, Canada, in 1610. He was a very kind man. He and his family taught Squanto the English language. He bought Squanto clothes and shoes to wear. Squanto became used to eating the white man's food and learned many of the white man's ways. He became one of Mr. Slaney's servants and was treated kindly. Mr. Slaney had a large house and many servants. He told Squanto that one day he may be sending a ship to the New World and if so, he would arrange the details so that Squanto could sail home.

Bound for Home

It was more than three years later when Mr. Slaney told Squanto that he knew the captain of a ship sailing for the New World. The captain needed someone to act as an **interpreter** so he could trade with the Native Americans. Squanto was excited.

He would finally get to see his family again! Squanto was grateful to Mr. Slaney and told him he would never forget his many kindnesses. He thanked him for being his friend and promised to be a friend to good white men as long as he lived.

> **interpreter:** One who translates speech

Late in 1619, Captain Thomas Dermer, with Squanto on board, sailed for America. Their first stop was far north of Squanto's home. Captain Dermer kept Squanto with him all through the winter and spring. He made many stops along the coast, trading with Native Americans for furs and salt fish. Squanto served as his interpreter as well as a peacemaker. Finally, by summer, the captain had his ship loaded with goods to take to England. Squanto and Captain Dermer said goodbye. He sailed down to Cape Cod and his men rowed Squanto to shore not far from his village. They waved goodbye, leaving Squanto on the shore.

A Silent Village

Squanto was so happy to be back home. He started on the path to his village. When he arrived, he was brokenhearted to find that it was deserted. No one was there. He was sick with grief as he walked the streets of the

Squanto — Friend of the Pilgrims

silent village. He bowed his head and prayed and cried. He decided he had to see the great chief Massasoit. He would know what had happened to his people. At last, he reached Massasoit's village and ran up to the great chief, stating that he was Squanto and he had been kidnapped and had lived in England for

several years. Massasoit told Squanto that a great plague had come two years ago. All of Squanto's people had died. They called it "The Great Dying." Historians think it was probably smallpox. He invited Squanto to live with his people and make their village his home. Squanto accepted.

The Pilgrims

It was less than a year later that Massasoit's scouts reported a great ship in the harbor. White men, women, and children were beginning to build on the site of Squanto's old village. Samoset, who knew a little English was sent to meet them. He walked into their settlement one day and said, "Welcome!" He told them about Squanto, who had lived with the English for several years. He promised to bring him to meet them soon. Massasoit sent Squanto to talk with the English to see if they were friendly. He and 60 braves were waiting in the nearby woods in case Squanto needed their help.

Samoset went with Squanto. They told the Pilgrims that the great Massasoit was waiting nearby to meet them. Myles Standish, the Pilgrim's main protector, requested he bring only 20 braves. He feared being greatly outnumbered because he was not sure he could trust them yet. Governor Bradford stepped forward and introduced himself to Squanto. Squanto liked him right away. Massasoit came to meet the Pilgrims and they agreed to make a peace treaty. Massasoit promised to warn them if any unfriendly neighboring tribes began to cause trouble. They agreed to help each other if that should happen. That night William Bradford came to Squanto and asked him to stay with the Pilgrims. Squanto liked the people so much, he felt he wanted to live with the Pilgrims indefinitely.

Squanto — Friend of the Pilgrims

Squanto Helps the Pilgrims

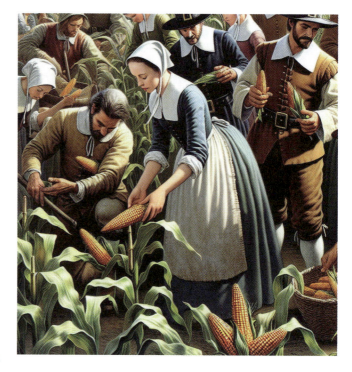

Squanto taught the Pilgrims many skills to help them survive in the New World. For instance, he told them corn must be planted when the leaves on the trees were the size of a mouse's ear. When planting he taught them to use a fish as fertilizer. He worked with them in the corn fields. He showed them how to fish with nets to catch many fish at one time. He showed them where to fish and how to hunt for beaver. Bradford said there was not "any amongst them that ever saw a beaver skin till they came here and were informed by Squanto."[7] He taught them the secrets of the forest. He showed them where to find sweet wild strawberries, and which plants were good for food.

When William Bradford's wife died, Squanto came to live in Bradford's house. Bradford relied heavily on Squanto. William Bradford called him "a special instrument sent of God for their good, beyond their expectation."[8] Bradford explained to Squanto how they had come to America for religious freedom. He talked to him frequently about God and Squanto listened as Bradford often prayed.

Squanto in Danger

One day, one of Massasoit's scouts came with a message for Squanto. Another tribe of Native Americans was very angry with Squanto for being the "white man's tongue" and arranging a treaty with Massasoit's tribe. He thought they may be preparing to go on the warpath. Squanto and the scout set out to check and see if the danger was imminent. On the trail, they met some braves who invited them to their village. The warriors in the village welcomed them until one of them recognized Squanto. They gathered around Squanto threatening to kill him. The scout saw Squanto was in danger, quietly slipped away, and ran to tell the Pilgrims.

Meanwhile, Squanto told the tribe that if they killed him, the white men would come with guns that roared louder than thunder. Those braves decided to see if the white men would come for Squanto. If they did not come, they would kill him. The scout got lost on the way to the

Pilgrim settlement. He finally arrived but got lost again guiding them to where Squanto was being held.

Squanto began to wonder if his friends would come for him after all. Squanto began to pray: "Help me, God... I am an Indian brave. The Pilgrims are my friends. I do not

Squanto — Friend of the Pilgrims

know the words they speak to you. But help me, God of the Pilgrims, help me."[9] At last, Squanto heard the roar of the guns. His friends had not forgotten him. The Native people who were guarding him were frightened and ran away. The rest of the warriors begged them not to shoot. William Bradford talked to them, and they all went home in peace. The Pilgrims rejoiced to see Squanto safe. They agreed they would not know what to do without Squanto. The Pilgrims got on their knees to thank God and Squanto joined them: "I must thank your God too. When you go to church, I shall go with you. I shall pray to your God. I shall worship Him as you do — all the rest of my life."[10]

The First Thanksgiving

Fall came. It was harvest time. Squanto helped gather in the corn. The people were thankful and wanted to set aside a day to thank God for all His blessings. They decided they would have a Thanksgiving feast. They invited Massasoit, who brought 90 warriors with him. The women and girls worked to prepare the food. Squanto and four of the men went hunting for wild game — turkeys, deer, geese, and ducks. The day finally came. Everyone had plenty to eat. After the feast, they ran races and played games. The Native people wanted to stay longer and went hunting to bring more meat. The Pilgrims counted their many blessings. They prayed and sang hymns of thanksgiving.

More Colonists

A ship from England soon arrived, carrying 35 more colonists. The Pilgrims welcomed them but were a bit concerned. They knew they would not have enough food now for the winter. Squanto went to see Massasoit and told him the Pilgrims needed more food. Massasoit had experienced a bountiful harvest and promised to send corn. Massasoit advised Squanto to leave soon and go to other neighboring tribes to trade for corn so the Pilgrims would have enough to last all winter. Winter was coming fast and it would soon be too cold. Captain Standish, ten men, and Squanto left to trade with other tribes. Arriving at a village they met Native Americans who had never seen white men. They offered them beads and gifts in exchange for corn. They were glad to make the trade. Now the Pilgrims would have enough food for the winter.

That night Squanto did not feel well. In the morning, he shook with chills and burned with a high fever. Bradford and the men cared for their friend, but Squanto knew he was going to die. He said he was not afraid. He asked them to pray for him. He wanted to go to their God in heaven. He took William Bradford's hand and said, "I have loved the Pilgrims well."[11] Squanto, the last of the Pawtuxet tribe, died. Squanto had only been with the Pilgrims for 20 months, but all of Plymouth agreed they would not have survived without their good and faithful friend.

4

William Bradford – Father of the Pilgrims

March 1590 – May 9, 1657

Who Was William Bradford?

William Bradford was born in Austerfield, England, in March 1590. His family owned several farms and raised sheep. His father died when William was only 16 months old. He grew up tending sheep, learning to plow and plant, and making hay. He also learned skills such as making butter and cheese, spinning wool, and handling the cattle. What he learned of farm life would be invaluable later to the Plymouth Colony.

Early Years

William's mother married again when he was four years old. William went to live with his grandfather. Two years later his grandfather died, and he went back to live with his mother and stepfather. However, after only a year his mother died. At seven years old, William was an orphan and went to live with his two uncles. William continued to work on the sheep farms they owned, but in a short time was afflicted, he later wrote, with "a soon and long illness."[12]

Though he had suffered much, William came to find this time a blessing nonetheless. Instead of shepherding, he had much time to read. His uncles, too, saw an advantage. William could help conduct the family business by drafting deeds and doing clerical work. William was able to get an education, probably from the local minister. Now William had access to **theological** books.

> **theological:** The study of God and His relationship to the world

46   Heroes of Early America

Of course, the Bible was one of the main books he read, as well as *Foxe's Book of Martyrs*. By age 12, he was thoroughly familiar with the Scriptures. William and his family had attended the **Anglican** church at Austerfield every Sunday ever since he could remember.

> **Anglican:** Official church of England

Puritan Ideas

From his Bible reading, William began to question if Queen Elizabeth's church was the only true church. When William was 12 years old, he met a friend his age who invited him to go to a Puritan church eight miles down the road in Babworth. An older man, Richard Clyfton, was preaching that the English church needed to be **reformed**. The Puritan thinking excited William. It seemed to be more in line with what he read in his Bible. His uncles were not happy, but William decided he must do what he felt was right. He enjoyed the simple services and the friendly people.

Halfway between his house and the Puritan church was Scrooby Manor, the home of William Brewster. William Brewster was 37 years old when he first met William Bradford.

> **reformed:** Improved

William Bradford — Father of the Pilgrims

He soon became a good friend, teacher, and even like a father to young William. They both had been questioning the English church. Brewster loaned William many books. Brewster could have lived in comfort. He had a government job with a good salary, but instead he chose to encourage pastors to rebuild their congregations based on the Word of God.

When King James took the throne, he made a law forbidding the Puritans to meet by themselves. He set out to destroy them. Some Puritans were thrown in prison and others were killed. Some had their homes **confiscated** and their money taken away. Mr. Brewster and a few men decided to start a new gathering at Scrooby. William felt welcome at the gatherings. People were allowed to ask questions and discuss the Bible freely. Members chose leaders from among themselves. This was never allowed in the Church of England. The king appointed those in charge and no questions were allowed.

confiscated: Seized

The Scrooby Separatists met secretly for about a year. Then King James made another new law requiring every person in England to attend the Church of England. If they did not, they would be put in jail. William's uncles began to put pressure on him to start attending the Church of England. They threatened to make him leave home if he did not comply. William loved his uncles and told them so, but he packed up his belongings and went to live with Mr. Brewster and his family. The king began to confiscate land and farm animals belonging to the Separatists. Many were arrested. Mr. Brewster was arrested one day, made to pay a huge fine, and told to stop talking about new ideas. Instead, he came up with a new idea. He encouraged the Scrooby group to move to Holland so they could worship God as they believed the Bible required them to do.

To Holland

As the Separatists were about to leave for Holland, King James' soldiers came and seized all their earthly possessions. The captain of the ship that they had hired to take them to Holland had tricked them. He had secretly turned them over to the king. The group was thrown in jail. Even from his jail cell, young William was firm in his beliefs. He determined he would get to Holland somehow. A month later, most of the Separatists were released. But now, what could

they do? They had sold their homes, and all their money had been stolen from them. They tried to find temporary homes. William stayed with the Brewster family again.

In the spring of 1608, they attempted again to get to Holland. The men walked 40 miles to get to the ship. The women and children went by flatboat. It got stuck in the mud, and they were not able to get to the ship. William Bradford stayed behind to help the women and children. The captain of the ship sailed away with the men. The English officials did not know what to do with the women and children who were crying for their husbands and fathers, so they let them go. They were able to leave in small groups to finally get to Holland.

William got a job as a weaver in Holland. He met and fell in love with Dorothy May. He had inherited some money from his family in England, and he bought a little house. He and Dorothy married when she turned 16 years old. In about a year, they had a little boy they named John. Things were going well for a while, but the Separatists became concerned about Holland's governmental **stability**. Holland was about to go to war with Spain, and if Spain won, Holland would be ruled by a king or queen. They would lose their freedom again. So, they began to talk about leaving Holland for America.

stability: Reliability

On to America

On September 20, 1620, William and Dorothy set sail for America onboard the *Mayflower*. The living quarters were crowded and many people were seasick. William grew to know and like many of the people who were not part of the Separatist group. He earned their respect, which he retained for the rest of his life. They felt he was someone they could trust to govern and make wise and just decisions. After two long, hard months they were overjoyed to see land. The first order of business before anyone could get off the ship was to write up a set of rules for how the colony would be governed. All the men agreed that everyone was equal and all decisions about the colony would be made as a group. They chose a man to be governor. Then they fell to their knees and gave thanks to God for bringing them safely across the ocean.

William was present on all the exploring trips led by Myles Standish. On one of these trips, William suddenly found himself upside down,  dangling from a tree. He had stepped on a deer trap that Native Americans had set. He laughed about it and told the story for years afterward. William was present when they sailed the boat along the coast and located the settlement at Plymouth. It had everything they

William Bradford — Father of the Pilgrims

were looking for — fresh water, a good port, and even cleared land. He was excited to get back and tell Dorothy. When he arrived, however, he was **horrified** to find out that Dorothy had fallen overboard and had drowned.

Winter Time

William did not have time to grieve. Construction had to be done. Once the common house was built, it was used as a hospital. William was one of the sick ones that winter. He hurt his hip so badly that he had a hard time standing. He was sick in the common house the night it caught on fire. Bundles of burning straw were falling on sick folks. He knew there were barrels of gunpowder that had to be moved and piles of muskets. William was well enough to get up but could not help much. As he watched the common house burn, he realized he had lost almost everything he owned, including his wife. Still, he had a deep sense that God would care for him.

horrified: Greatly distressed

When Squanto came to live with the Pilgrims, he moved in with Bradford. They became best friends. Both had lost their homes and loved ones and learned to live with sorrow. William later wrote that Squanto was "a special instrument sent of God for their good."[13] He also wrote, "Squanto continued with them and was their interpreter.... He directed them how to set their corne, where to take fish, and to procure other commodities, and was also their pilot to bring them to unknown places for their profit, and never left them till he died."[14]

Governor Bradford

In April 1621, Governor John Carver suddenly died. The men voted William Bradford as the next governor to guide them. William prayed to God for guidance; God certainly directed them and blessed them. By October, they finished building all the houses. They traded with Native Americans for many beaver pelts to send back to England to help pay off their debt. The corn was ready to harvest. William wanted to find a special way to thank God. He declared a holiday of Thanksgiving and invited Massasoit and his braves to come. The braves brought meat, and there was food enough to last for three days of celebration. The Pilgrims and Native Americans ate and played games and grew to be better friends.

William Bradford — Father of the Pilgrims

Father to the Pilgrims

More colonists arrived from England. William had heard that Alice Southworth whom he had known in Holland, had become a widow. He wrote asking her to come to Plymouth to marry him. In the summer of 1623, she arrived on a ship with her two little boys and her sister's family.

During their marriage, Alice and William raised many children. They had three of their own children. Then there was John, the son born to William and Dorothy, Alice's two children from her first marriage, and her nephew. In addition to these children, they took care of four Pilgrim children who had been orphaned. William was always ready to help his Pilgrim family members.

As time passed, William Bradford became a happy landowner and family man. He taught all his children how to read and write. The children were delighted to hear the stories of God's provision and guidance for the Pilgrims. William knew he should write the story down for others. It took him 20 years to write *Of Plymouth Plantation*, which is still widely read today. It testifies to the gracious hand of a loving God who faithfully cared for His courageous people and carried them through many a trial.

William Bradford was elected governor 31 times during his lifetime. He refused to be paid. He had a strong belief that God had given him all he possessed, and he, in turn, would give to others. He was looked upon as a kind father to all. He helped settle many disputes judiciously. He worked diligently along with several others of the men to pay off the Pilgrims' debt to the financiers in England who had loaned them money for the journey.

William Bradford was a wise governor who loved his people and put their interests first. He made sure each man got an equal share of land. He insisted that the people were to vote for their leaders. When food was scarce, he carefully distributed equal amounts to all. He kept the church from ruling the people. If people who were not Separatists wanted to join the church, they were welcome, but not pressured to do so. "The Pilgrim vision of church life would last to the present time and give rise to thousands and thousands of congregations that would choose their own ministers and their way of worship."[15]

William Bradford — Father of the Pilgrims

William's ideas of liberty for all were the seed of thought that shaped the American government. When William Bradford died in 1657, the Pilgrims mourned the loss of their beloved friend. William Bradford, though he never knew his own father, would be pleased to know he is remembered as the Father of the Pilgrims.

5

Pocahontas – Powhatan Princess

Circa 1596 – March 1617

Who Was Pocahontas?

Pocahontas was born in the village of Werowocomoco, the area that later became Jamestown, Virginia. Her father was Powhatan, chief of the Powhatan tribe. She was named Matoaka (Little Snow Feather), but later she was nicknamed Pocahontas, meaning "Playful One." No one knows when she was born or exactly who her mother was. The chief of the tribe had a large family. The women all helped to raise the children. Young girls were taught by the women how to gather wood, plant and care for gardens, make clay pottery vessels for cooking, weave baskets, make beadwork, make simple clothing from animal skins, and of course, watch younger children. Pocahontas was clearly her father's favorite daughter. She probably did not have to do much work. Other children worked much and played little, but for Pocahontas, it was much play and little work. Because of her royal position, her family had servants to grow their food and make their clothes. She had lots of free time to explore the woods, swim in the river, and hunt for shells.

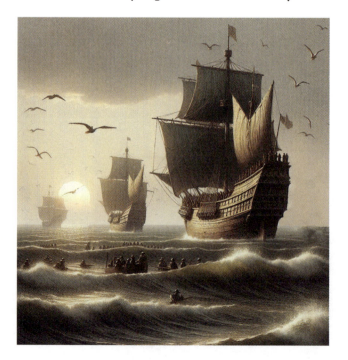

Ships Arrive

In April 1607, three ships arrived from England. They carried 100 men and four boys who were coming to start a colony

Heroes of Early America

in the New World. They had brought five months' worth of food and supplies with them. They brought grain, hogs, and salted meat, along with guns and ammunition and a small boat that could be assembled once they arrived. They did not realize, however, that they had landed right in the middle of Powhatan's tribal hunting grounds.

The area was covered with thick vines that had to be cleared before they could build homes. Drinking water was scarce. Much of the water was mixed with salt water and therefore, could not be used for drinking. Other water sources were contaminated. The settlers used the river for drinking water; it was also used for bathing and washing dirty clothes. The potential for germs causing illness was likely. The men were so happy to be on land that they did not consider all these things. By mid-August, nearly half of the colony had died. They began to build a fort for protection. All who were able pitched in to help with the work.

Relations between the English and the Native Americans were uncertain. Powhatan agreed to trade goods with the white men, but he did not trust them. He brought corn and other food, and exchanged them for tools, beads, and European goods. This helped the colonists tremendously as their food supply was getting low. Pocahontas was

12 years old and quite curious. She took time to befriend the English soon after they landed.

Smith, while leading an exploring party, had wandered too far into Powhatan's land. Those with Smith were immediately killed by Powhatan's warriors. Smith pulled a compass from his pocket and offered it to the braves.

The moving dial fascinated them. It made them wonder if Smith was a great chief. They decided to take him to their chief Powhatan, instead of killing him on the spot. Smith was held captive for weeks. Pocahontas heard about this white man who was possibly a chief. She was very curious to see him.

John Smith's first meeting with Pocahontas was **providential**. Smith later said that at first he was welcomed by the great chief and a feast was given in his honor, even though he was actually a captive. Pocahontas attended the feast at her father's house and met Captain John Smith personally. Using signs, Powhatan asked Smith why he and his men had come. He asked how long they planned to stay. Powhatan told him the land belonged to him. It was his great hunting grounds. Then Powhatan spoke to his warriors.

providential: Fortunate, determined by God

All of sudden, Smith was grabbed and forced to stretch out on the ground. About 200 warriors lined up to **gawk at** Smith. They placed his head on a large stone. Standing all around Smith, they began waving clubs and chanting. Suddenly, young Pocahontas ran to her father, begging him not to kill Smith. At first, he would not listen to her, so she came to Smith, taking his head in her arms. At this, Powhatan agreed to let him live. Having been saved by a member of Powhatan's family gave the braves a new respect for John Smith.

gawk at: To stare or observe

John Smith and Pocahontas began to develop a friendly relationship. Smith was very fond of the girl. She learned some English words. and they worked on a system of communication. Smith was now considered a member of the family. Powhatan treated him as a son. Pocahontas regarded him as a brother.

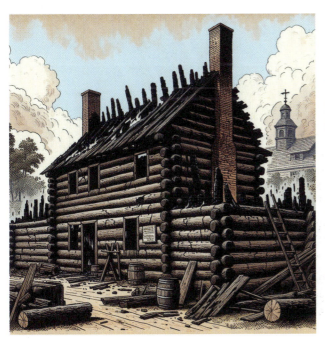

Return to the Fort

Finally, John Smith was allowed to return to the fort. The next winter was hard for the colonists. The people had very little food; a fire burned down part of the fort. Powhatan decided to help the English. Pocahontas came with baskets of food and meat. Without her help, the settlers would have died

Pocahontas — Powhatan Princess

that winter. Pocahontas visited the fort often. The men gave her many presents like pretty beads and even a mirror. She played games with the boys and often talked with John Smith. She kept learning to speak English.

John Smith later commented that "it was the ordinance of God to make her thus His instrument."[16] According to Smith, she was "*next, under God ... the instrument to preserve this colony from death, famine, and utter confusion.*"[17]

When John Smith left to go on an expedition to explore new lands, other men carried on the leadership within the English settlement. The Native Americans didn't trust them, though. A few situations developed that caused Powhatan to not feel as friendly toward the English. Pocahontas, however, saved the English settlers from planned attacks by the Native Americans. Pocahontas seemed to feel like the white settlers were family to John Smith, and he was family to her. She made many efforts to help preserve peace and tranquility between the settlers and her tribe. Pocahontas continued to make visits to Jamestown, bringing food to the settlers. John Smith had a bad accident. Gunpowder exploded near him, burning him seriously. He knew recovery would be long and hard. Therefore, he went back to England on October 1, 1609.

Kidnapped

In 1613, a man named Samuel Argall came on a trading mission to the Jamestown colony. He was not a good man. Hearing that Pocahontas lived nearby, he decided to try to **kidnap** her. He wanted to get Powhatan to release his men whom Powhatan had taken prisoner in exchange for getting his daughter back. He also wanted stolen guns returned, and he demanded a promise of peace. He got help from another Native American chief who was not friendly

kidnap: Take someone away illegally

with Powhatan. The chief agreed to have his wife coax Pocahontas to go aboard the ship with her to dine with the captain and his friends. Pocahontas agreed. After the meal, she was locked into a room on the ship. Powhatan did release the prisoners but would not return guns and had no intention of making peace with Argall. Powhatan requested that his daughter not be mistreated. Governor Thomas Gates, the colonial governor of Jamestown, was fearful of **reprisal** by Powhatan, and made sure Pocahontas was treated well. She was a type of **celebrity** among the colonists. After all, she was a princess.

Introduction to Christianity

Pocahontas was taken to Henrico, the colony's second settlement. Here she was taught by Reverend Alexander Whitaker about the Christian faith. One of the goals of the Virginia Company, which established the new colonies, was to teach the Christian religion to the natives. She lived on the 100-acre **parsonage**.

reprisal: Revenge

celebrity: Famous person

parsonage: House and lands provided for a preacher

Pocahontas — Powhatan Princess

There, she received instruction in English ways of dress, speech, and manners. Perhaps she felt **abandoned** by her father, or perhaps she just appreciated the kindness with which she was treated. At any rate, she readily learned and adopted instruction in the Bible and in the English way of life. She memorized all the prayers of the Church of England and became fluent in English. An 18th-century historian wrote that she "expressed an eager desire and showed great capacity in learning."[18] She seemed to prefer the English way of life over the Native American culture. She enjoyed the English style of dress. Soon she attracted the notice of a 28-year-old widower.

abandoned: Left alone

John Rolfe had lost his wife and baby daughter a few years earlier. He was a farmer. He met Pocahontas in church. He helped her with her prayers and studies. Their relationship continued to grow. Rolfe wrote a letter to the acting governor of the colony expressing his desire to marry Pocahontas. Everyone in the colony thought this was a great idea. Perhaps joining in marriage would help to unite the two cultures and bring peace. Word reached the now 80-year-old Powhatan of John Rolfe's desire to marry his daughter. He spoke of peace and offered to return weapons he had stolen from the English. He gave Pocahontas several pieces of land and a string of freshwater beads as a wedding gift.

Pocahontas Becomes a Christian

Pocahontas accepted the Christian faith as her own. She gave up her Native American spiritual heritage and embraced the teachings of Jesus Christ. She insisted on being baptized prior to her wedding day. A massive painting of the baptism of Pocahontas is hanging in the U.S. Capitol building. She took the name of Rebecca and began her new life. She and John Rolfe were married in 1614. With their wedding, there began an eight-year period named the Peace of Pocahontas. Powhatan agreed to live in peace with the colonists. Pocahontas enjoyed helping her new husband with his farming. She knew many helpful tips she had learned as a girl. For instance, she told him how to plant fish for fertilizer and that young plants grew better when planted with exposure to the south. Within a year, John and Rebecca had a baby son named Thomas.

Visit to England

Governor Thomas Dale, the deputy governor of Jamestown, wanted to create interest in England about the new colonies. He was planning to go to London and invited the Rolfe family to go with him. Pocahontas would see London, and the English people would have the chance to meet a real Native American princess. The Virginia Company offered a yearly income to Pocahontas in appreciation for her willingness to travel by ship to England. John Rolfe was Secretary of the Virginia

Colony, and he would promote Jamestown to the English. They would gain support for the Virginia colony, as well as raise money to establish a school for Powhatan children. Pocahontas, as might be expected of a princess, planned to take an **entourage** of a dozen Native Americans with her. Her sister was one of

the people who came along to help care for baby Thomas.

The journey to England was difficult due to seasickness, so the group was delighted to finally see land appear. It must have been amazing to see the city with buildings, carriages, and people everywhere. One of the Native Americans traveling with them later told Powhatan that there were as many English "as the stars in the sky, the sand on the English beaches, or the leaves on the trees."[19] Pocahontas was introduced to many members of the English **aristocracy**. Admired for her charm, grace, and intelligence, Pocahontas was treated as the daughter of a king. She had many invitations to fancy dinners and parties.

entourage: A group of people attending to the needs of an important person

aristocracy: Nobility

John Smith

Pocahontas had thought John Smith to be dead, but he heard she was in England, and he came to visit her there. She was so surprised to see him she could not speak for a few minutes. He had recently returned from an expedition to New England. He had written a long letter to Queen Anne of England praising Pocahontas' character, telling how she had rescued them so many times. Pocahontas said to John Smith, "…I will be forever and ever your countryman."[20]

Soon the damp, cold air of London began to affect some of the Native Americans. Two of them died. John Rolfe moved them out of London to the countryside, thinking the clear air would help. But by that time, Pocahontas had developed a cough. People now think it may have been the beginning of tuberculosis. Rebecca loved the countryside in England and would have stayed there, but John Rolfe's business was back in Virginia.

Last Days

Baby Thomas was ill now, too. John felt he must take his family back to Virginia. They set sail in March. John believed their health would surely improve soon. Rebecca and Thomas went to the sleeping quarters to rest as the ship left

port. When they were only 25 miles out, though, it became evident that Pocahontas could not travel farther. John Rolfe requested they be dropped off in the town of Gravesend. He called the local doctor. Unfortunately, nothing could be done. The doctor thought she was suffering from bleeding in her lungs. Pocahontas, even though dying, was thinking of others. She told her husband, "All must die. 'Tis enough that the child liveth."[21]

A Christian funeral was held, and Rebecca Rolfe was buried at St. George's church in Gravesend, England. Today a bronze statue of the beloved Powhatan princess stands in the churchyard. Another one just like it stands in Jamestown, Virginia. Her son did survive, although John had to leave him in the care of a guardian who lived in England as he was too sick to make the journey.

The peace of Pocahontas lasted for another year until Powhatan died. The short life of Pocahontas serves as an inspiration for many. She took numerous risks to put the interests of others before her own. Because of her influence, the greatest period of peace between Native Americans and the English settlers at that time was established.

6

John Alden – Pillar of Strength

Circa 1599 – September 12, 1687

Who Was John Alden?

John Alden, the son of a minister, was born in London, England. Not much is known about his early life. He was orphaned when very young. Historians think he may have been schooled by John Alden, a lawyer of Hertfordshire, who was most likely his uncle. He was the youngest signer of the *Mayflower* Compact and rose to have a leadership role in the Plymouth Colony. He played a prominent part in the colony's affairs. Robert Alden was one of a group of merchants called "The London Adventurers." Together they financed the *Mayflower's* voyage. John likely heard of the group of Pilgrims from this relative.

The Trade of a Cooper

The profession of a cooper was a good job for someone who liked the sea and was skilled in working with wood. A cooper was a barrel maker. Barrels were used for holding important food and cargo. It took seven years for an apprentice to learn the trade. Barrels had to be made without any flaws and a good cooper had to be able to produce two barrels each day. The barrels were crafted having an exact curve in the wood, precise fittings, and hoops tightly secured so they would not leak.

English law required any ship sailing from English ports to have a cooper onboard. His job was to make sure the barrels were stored properly. They could not roll around when the ship was tossed about in the waves. The cooper also had to keep the

Heroes of Early America

barrels in good repair on a long voyage. If he failed in his job, it could cause great loss to the ship owner as well as to passengers relying on the stored goods for survival. "It can truly be said that the success of any voyage depends as much upon the ship's cooper as upon her captain."[22]

John Alden — Cooper

John Alden was 21 years old when he was hired by Captain Christopher Jones in Southampton, England. He served as the cooper during the *Mayflower's* voyage to America. He signed on to get the ship's goods safely to America. After that, he could go back to England if he wished. At Southampton, John met William Brewster and John Carver. They were leaders of a group of people called Separatists, who had left England to worship freely. They were in Holland, awaiting the voyage of the *Mayflower*. He also met Captain Myles Standish, a soldier who had been hired to protect the traveling Pilgrims.

John worked to fill barrels with oatmeal, flour, salt, beans, cabbages, butter, peas, salt beef, and a type of bread known as ship biscuit. Food and provisions had to be packed carefully. Myles Standish helped to pack things like muskets, ammunition, and cutlasses; he even had two cannons. Pots, pans, dishes, candle molds, nets, fishing equipment, carpentry tools, and gardening tools were all needed for establishing a settlement in the New World. A shoemaker, William Mullins, gave John several barrels full of shoes and shoemaking supplies. Mr. Mullins was bringing his family along with him. People who knew the trades, such as carpentry, blacksmithing, leather work, and many others, were needed to successfully build a community in the New World. The people on the *Mayflower* who were not Separatists were called Strangers. Later, all the passengers became known as the Pilgrims.

Off to the New World

By August 1620, the ship was outfitted and ready to sail. They set off on September 6, 1620, with many unknowns ahead of them. Captain Jones was in command of the ship and was well-experienced. He had commanded the *Mayflower* for 12 years. It was actually a cargo ship, not meant to carry passengers. All 102 passengers were crowded between the hold and the upper deck. There was only five feet of headroom, so a tall person couldn't even stand up straight. The crew lived in a different part of the

Heroes of Early America

ship. The weather was nice for several days, but then heavy storms came. This made John's job incredibly difficult. The tossing of the ship damaged some of the barrels and he had to repair them.

John was the only crew member who came in close contact with the passengers. He got to know many of the passengers. He especially noticed Priscilla Mullins, the shoemaker's daughter. Her cheerful spirit encouraged many. People began to get sick as time went on. Many were seasick. John was amazed at the patience of the Separatists. They read their Bible regularly, prayed often, and did not complain. He admired their courage.

Land Ho

After 68 days at sea, on November 9, 1620, the ship's lookout sighted land. Captain Jones was not sure where they were. They had planned to land on the coast of northern Virginia but had been blown off course by the storms. He determined they were off the coast of Cape Cod, much farther north than planned. Rather than try to find their way back to their original destination, however, they decided to look for a good place to land since winter would soon be upon them. Before they **disembarked**, the Pilgrims drew up a document which had rules for the government of their colony. Most of the men signed it and agreed to abide by the rules. John Alden was the seventh man to sign. The document was *The Mayflower* Compact. Mr. John Carver was elected to be governor. The next morning they approached Provincetown at the tip of Cape Cod. The long journey was over, and the Pilgrims fell upon their knees to offer thanks to God for bringing them safely across the ocean.

disembarked: Left the ship

shallop: A light wooden boat used as a rowboat

The **shallop** was a boat the Pilgrims brought to help explore the inlets. It had been badly damaged on the trip. John Alden, with his great carpentry skill, set about to repair the damage. Provisions had gotten a bit low, and John carefully checked the barrels and casks. Exploring parties went out for several days and finally chose Plymouth Harbor as a suitable place to settle.

The Long Winter

On December 23, some of the Pilgrims took their tools and went ashore to start building. The first structure they worked on was a common house. John Alden divided his time between land and

Heroes of Early America

shore. He was sleeping on the ship since he was a member of the crew and planned to return to England when the year was over. John had to carefully watch the provisions, and he also helped the men on shore with the construction. It was growing colder and some of the settlers were getting sick.

Once the common house was finished, the men started on the houses for the Pilgrims. When Myles Standish's wife died of the sickness, John left the ship to live with Myles. The winter was almost over, but sickness continued. Mr. and Mrs. Mullins and their son Joseph all died. Now Priscilla was alone. She found comfort in the Lord. She went to live with the Brewster family, who welcomed her into their home. All but four women had died that winter. Priscilla was busy caring for the sick, mending, washing clothes, cooking, and being a mother to orphaned children. Priscilla's admiration for John Alden grew daily. He was gentle and kind and was always singing. He often led the children in a song to cheer them. She knew he planned to go back to England when the year ended, so she tried to not get too fond of the times he would stop and talk to her.

The *Mayflower* Sails Back to England

Spring had come and the Mayflower was due to sail back to England in a week. John **contemplated** what he should do. He knew in his heart that his skills were needed at Plymouth. The Pilgrims' numbers had decreased, and he was a crucial part of the colony, developing a love for the Pilgrims and their ways. Each Sunday he had worshiped with them, and so this helped him decide to stay. He would protect Priscilla Mullins.

> **contemplated:** Thought about

When a small Pilgrim boy by the name of Johnny Billington was found missing, the Pilgrims asked the friendly Native American chief Massasoit if he knew where the boy was. Massasoit said he had heard Johnny was with the Nauset tribe. John Alden and some other volunteers set out in the shallop to look for him. John brought corn to give to the Nauset chief. The Nausets had treated Johnny well. They agreed that they would be at peace with the Pilgrims. In November 1621, three days were set aside for a time to thank God for His bountiful blessings to them all. Massasoit was invited and he came, bringing many braves. Priscilla and the other women scurried to cook more food. Massasoit sent braves to get meat to share.

Heroes of Early America

More Colonists

Some months later, a ship arrived from England with 35 newcomers who wanted to join the group. The ship was named the *Fortune*, sent by the London Adventures who had financed the Pilgrim's voyage. The captain of this ship dropped off his passengers and set sail to return to England. John and Priscilla stood watching it.

They were free to return with the ship if they chose to. John knew in his heart that he would never go back to England. He had become one of the Pilgrims. Priscilla asked him if he were glad he stayed. He answered, "Yes, Priscilla. My place is here with you."[23] John and Priscilla were married later that summer by Mr. Brewster. He told John, "We are thankful you chose to remain with us. You are strong and you set yourself to any task that needs to be done. Such an attitude helps our colony to survive."[24] John built a small house for him and Priscilla in the town square.

John's Generous Offer

The Pilgrims still needed to pay their debt to the London Adventurers. John Alden was now a very important and respected man in Plymouth. He proposed an idea at a town meeting. He heard that the

Abnaki Native Americans who lived in northern New England had many furs to trade, and he suggested setting up a trading post. Then the money they earned could pay the debt.

The fall harvest was plentiful, and the governor approved the idea of a trading post. John Alden manned one of the shallops and led the trading party to the Kennebec River. Here they traded corn for four hundred pounds of furs. An arrangement was made with the London Adventurers. The Pilgrims would pay 1,800 pounds of fur in exchange for the Adventurers giving up their claim on the land and property. Nine men were placed in charge of the trading. John Alden was one of them. They called themselves the "undertakers," meaning they were undertaking the task of paying the colony's debt themselves. They built a trading post at Augusta, Maine, and for many years had profitable trade relations with the Abnakis. In time, the debt to the Adventurers was paid off. The colony grew and prospered.

Duxbury

Other towns were springing up around Plymouth. John and Priscilla had three children by that time. They moved to a farm in Duxbury, ten miles away. The Aldens named it Eagle Tree Farm. The Standishes moved to

Duxbury as well. They were neighbors and their children played together. While Priscilla cooked supper each evening, John read to his children from the Bible. After supper, the children would beg him to tell stories about the voyage on the *Mayflower* and the hard winter. The Aldens had six more children. One of their daughters married one of Myles Standish's sons.

John Alden and Myles Standish helped to survey new towns. John wanted to see a canal constructed to save ships from having to sail around the tip of the Cape. Nearly 300 years later in 1909, this canal was started: the Cape Cod Canal.

A Life of Service

John Alden served the Plymouth Colony unselfishly for many more years. He was made a **magistrate** and performed marriages. From 1640 to 1650, he was Treasurer of the town of Duxbury. He assisted on the governor's board for 53 years. He was made deputy governor, and at the age of 80, was senior assistant to the governor. He also served on the Council of War. He served on the home guard during

magistrate: Civilian judge

John Alden — Pillar of Strength

King Philip's War. This had been a war between the Native Americans and the colonists started by a son of Massasoit after his father's death, to drive the English from the land. The English won the war, but there was much property damage. John served on the council to help rebuild after that war.

The Aldens were active in the Congregational Church established by the Pilgrims. John's Bible is still preserved in the Pilgrim Hall Museum in Plymouth, Massachusetts. When John and Priscilla grew old, they moved in with their son Jonathan. This house still stands today — the only one of the Pilgrim homes still standing. John was 87 when he died in 1687. He was the last survivor of the signers of *The Mayflower* Compact. Priscilla lived a few more years.

Of the *Mayflower* passengers, John and Priscilla had the most descendants. They were parents of 11 children, each of whom embraced the Christian faith. They had 69 grandchildren and nearly 500 great-grandchildren. Today, there are estimated to be over a million Alden descendants. Just as a pillar holds up a building, John Alden was a pillar to the Pilgrims whose goal was to establish a colony in the New World that would bring glory to God.

7

William Penn – Defender of Religious Freedom

October 14, 1644 – July 30, 1718

Who Was William Penn?

At the time of William Penn's birth, England was embroiled in a civil war that had been going on for two years. King Charles I and his **Royalist** army were fighting against Oliver Cromwell and **Parliament**. Oliver Cromwell had the position of Lord Protector of England.

This meant he was a Parliamentary commander in England, but not a member of the royal family. The king believed he had total power to rule the people. Cromwell and Parliament were representatives elected by the people. They believed they had the power to make laws to limit the king's power. William entered the world during this time of turmoil.

> **Royalist:** Those who support rule by a king
>
> **Parliament:** The ruling body of England

Early Years

William Penn was born on October 14, 1644, in London, England. William's father, also named William, was an officer in the British Navy. He supported King Charles I, but he also believed it was his duty to protect his country from attacks, no matter who was in power at the time. When Oliver Cromwell gained control of the British Navy in 1644, Captain Penn served under him. Cromwell promoted him to vice admiral. As such, Vice Admiral Penn was often at sea. Care of his children, William and Margaret, was left to their mother, the Vice Admiral's wife Margaret. In those days, London was a large, filthy city. When William was three he came down with the dreaded disease of **smallpox**. He survived, but as a result, he was bald for the rest of his life and often wore a wig to cover his head.

The Family Moves

While home on leave, William Penn's father decided to move his family out of the big city to a country home. They moved to Wanstead, which was ten miles from London. William spent most of his growing-up years here, enjoying the woods and being outdoors. The English Civil War was over in 1649. Cromwell had won and Parliament made him its leader. King Charles I was tried in court, found guilty, and **executed**. His son, Charles II, managed to escape to Holland. Admiral Penn was rewarded for his great victories at sea. Cromwell gifted him with land near Cork, Ireland, which included Macroom Castle. However, he chose to stay in England for the time being.

William started his education at Chigwell Free School. It was four miles away, and

smallpox: A contagious viral disease

executed: Put to death

William Penn — Defender of Religious Freedom

William would walk the distance six days a week to study. He was a good student. School started at 6:00 every morning with teaching and prayers, then Greek and English lessons. They stopped for a lunch break at 11:00, then resumed studies at 1:00 for English grammar, Latin, spelling, and moral training.

William learned to write and speak **Latin** by age 11.

Trouble

In 1655, Cromwell sent Admiral Penn and his men to capture Hispaniola, a large island in the West Indies. Admiral Penn and a fellow general found the fighting much more difficult than expected. The natives hid in the forest and shot arrows at the British soldiers. The British couldn't see where they were to fire back, so they abandoned that order. Instead, they captured the island of Jamaica, which proved easier to accomplish. Cromwell, however, was furious that his **directives** hadn't been obeyed. He ordered Admiral Penn and the other commanding officer to be sent to the Tower of London. This was an ancient fortress that was being used as a

Latin: The main language used by schools, churches, and the state in Europe

directives: Orders

prison. After five weeks in prison, Admiral Penn was released with the **stipulation** that he apologize to Cromwell, and he would not be allowed to go back to sea. The family returned to their home in Wanstead. William's mother was expecting another baby and his father decided

> **stipulation:**
> Condition

as soon as the baby was born, they would move to their castle in Ireland. William continued his studies at home in Ireland with a tutor.

Introduction to a Quaker

When William was 13 years old, his father invited a Quaker preacher, Thomas Loe, to their castle home. William had heard of the religious group and how they got their name. When a magistrate had threatened to sentence the Quaker leader to prison, he said, "Thee will learn to quake before the word of the Lord."[25] The magistrate, making fun of him, called the group the Quakers. The name stuck.

Admiral Penn gathered all the servants and family to hear Loe speak. He was a mild-mannered, kind man. He spoke of how religion wasn't a matter of outward observances, but a personal relationship: "Each man, in the quiet of his heart, must come to his own reckoning with God. For the Scriptures tell us that man looks on the outward appearance, but God looks at a man's heart."[26] William hadn't heard anything like this before. As Reverend Loe spoke, William noticed tears in his father's eyes. He had never seen his father cry before. The message was moving. William had been praying to God for a couple of years now, but he had never told anyone before. Now Reverend

Loe was telling them a person didn't need a priest to access God on his or her behalf. This encouraged William. He began reading and studying the Bible on his own.

Back to England

Oliver Cromwell died in 1658, and William's father moved the family back to England. Charles II was restored to the throne of his late father. He made Admiral Penn a knight. William began attending Oxford University. He participated in daily chapel services that were part of the Church of England, the only religion allowed in Britain. William had been studying the Word on his own. He also attended meetings at the home of the former dean of the university. The dean talked about independent thinking. He described people living together in freedom and deciding on laws to govern themselves. William began to question some of the external rules at Oxford and decided there were rules he could not follow. He was soon **expelled** from Oxford.

Parliament passed several laws against Quakers around that time, two of which were particularly **egregious** and unusually cruel. The first one was called the Quaker Act. It prevented Quakers from meeting in groups of more than five people. First-time offenders were fined, repeat offenders imprisoned, and those who refused to forsake their beliefs would be shipped to Jamaica and sold as slaves. The second law required all ministers in England and Wales to use the Church of England's *Book of Common Prayer*. There were about 2,000 ministers who chose to quit rather than follow this law. William was astounded. Charles II had promised to be tolerant of religious groups but had been outvoted by Parliament, including William's own father.

> **expelled:** Made to leave
>
> **egregious:** Obviously bad

William's father, ashamed of his son's beliefs, sent him to Paris,

hoping his son would learn the ways of the French court. Although William enjoyed his time there, he was more interested in religious freedom. He enrolled in the Academy of Saumur in western France which taught freedom of religion and tolerance of the beliefs of others.

William Penn — Defender of Religious Freedom 87

In 1665, William returned to England and enrolled in law school at the Inns of Court in London. While there, the **bubonic plague** spread throughout the city. It was so bad the school closed. Thousands of people died. William witnessed the great kindness and bravery of the Quakers who helped those afflicted by the plague when no one else would. They brought food to the sick, tended them, and took orphans into their homes. This was faith in action, William decided.

King Charles II gave William's father a larger estate and castle in Ireland. William went to manage it for him. While there, he learned that Thomas Loe was preaching again. He eagerly went to hear him. "It was at this time that the Lord visited me with … testimony of his eternal word."[27] William spent many hours talking with Thomas. He decided to become a Quaker.

> **bubonic plague:** A serious, usually fatal, infection spread by fleas

Imprisonments

William Penn's decision came with great consequences. He and his fellow Quakers were arrested while holding a meeting. This was the first of several imprisonments William suffered for his faith. William wrote a long letter to the authorities explaining that Quakers were not a political group, but a religious group committed to nonviolence. They therefore posed no threat to the government. He sent the letter to the **earl** of the province. **Consequently**, the prisoners were released. When he returned home, William's father told him he was an embarrassment. He ordered him to pack his clothes and leave home.

William continued to fight for religious freedom through speeches, writing, and debates. He was arrested a second time by the bishop of England for his writings and thrown in the Tower of London. The bishop offered to release him if he would **recant**. His response was, "My prison shall be my grave before I will budge a jot."[28] William wrote another tract explaining that his intent was not to attack the beliefs of the Church of England, and he was released.

> **earl:** British nobleman
>
> **consequently:** As a result
>
> **recant:** Publicly withdraw his belief

In 1671, William again went to prison. He refused to take an oath that said he would not take up arms against the king. William appealed, asking why was that even necessary when Quakers believed in nonviolence toward everyone? He was released six months later.

In April 1672, William Penn married a Quaker girl, Gulielma Springett, who became the joy of his life. In 1675, two Quakers who owned land in the colony of New Jersey, across the Atlantic Ocean, asked him to settle a dispute between them. He did and then

William Penn — Defender of Religious Freedom

helped them draw up a plan of government for the colony. It provided religious freedom for all and placed power in the hands of the people.

An Idea

William worked tirelessly for Quakers. He traveled to Germany, Holland, and Ireland, fighting to get laws changed. He dreamed of a new colony to be home to thousands of Quakers. Then he had an idea. King Charles II's brother owed Admiral Penn, who had recently died, a huge sum of money. William approached the **duke** to ask for land in America as payment for the debt. This pleased the duke, as it not only fulfilled his debt but would get rid of the troublesome

duke: A male ruler in England

Quakers in the process. On March 4, 1681, William Penn was given 46,000 square miles of land in British North America. King Charles named the land Pennsylvania in honor of his late friend, William's father. "Sylvan" means forest land in Latin. William said Pennsylvania would be a "holy experiment" where people could live in freedom to follow their beliefs with no fear of punishment.

Pennsylvania

William Penn set about planning for the colony. Over the years, he had made many contacts by fighting for religious freedom and encouraged Quakers from various countries to move to the colony.

He also wrote **tracts** encouraging skilled workers to move there, regardless of their religious beliefs, well aware that homes and shops would have to be built for them. He offered land at reasonable prices. He appointed his cousin to serve as deputy governor until he could get there himself. He instructed his cousin to establish good relations with Native Americans and settlers already living there. Together, they chose **Philadelphia** as a good location to establish a seaport town. Soon the population began to grow.

Penn worked to write a constitution for Pennsylvania to assure justice and freedom for all citizens, regardless of their religious beliefs. He organized the governing body into three parts. The council made the laws. The General Assembly voted on laws, and a governor would manage the colony. William Penn became the first governor. All men who owned property had the right to vote. They also elected members of the council and general assembly. Amendments could be added if ⅞ of the legislature and governor approved them. Individual rights of freedom of religion, freedom of the press, and trial by jury

tracts: Pamphlets

Philadelphia: Meaning "the city of brotherly love"

William Penn — Defender of Religious Freedom

were among those protected. Native Americans had equal rights. No taxes could be collected without the approval of the voters.

After making preparations for a year, William was ready to move to Pennsylvania. His wife was expecting their fourth child and planned to come later. The voyage took two months. An outbreak of smallpox onboard the ship killed 31 passengers. William had smallpox as a child, so he was **immune** and helped care for others. The ship arrived on October 27, 1682. The very next day William began to develop good relationships with the Native Americans. He insisted that they be treated with fairness and respect. He visited their villages, ate with them, learned their language, and even ran races with them. He insisted that no land be taken from them unless they wished to sell it.

> **immune:** Having antibodies to avoid getting the disease

Boundary Disputes

Some boundary disputes arose with Lord Baltimore of Maryland. After two years, William had to return to England along with Lord Baltimore to get things settled. He hated to leave and wrote a farewell letter to Pennsylvania: "My love & my life is to you & with you & no waters can quench it nor distance wear it out or bring it to an end."[29] In just three years, the population of Pennsylvania grew to more than 7,000 people. They had come from Wales, England,

Ireland, Holland, Sweden, and Germany. Trade was booming. The new government Penn had established was serving the people well.

William was delighted to be reunited with his family. Four months after he arrived in England, King Charles II had a stroke and died. The new king settled the border dispute in Penn's favor. He also released more than 1,300 Quaker prisoners. Then more unrest occurred in England. A new king took the throne and hardships prevented William from returning to Pennsylvania for years.

Back to Pennsylvania

On December 1, 1699, William and his family arrived in Chester, Pennsylvania. He had been gone for more than five years. An admiring crowd, including Native Americans, flocked to welcome him. He visited Philadelphia the next day and was astounded to see a thriving shipping port. It was now the second-largest city in America, with a population of 25,000. Streets were lined with pretty trees, stately brick homes, shops, schools, and churches. It had greatly prospered in 20 years since its founding.

William had much business to attend to. He again visited Native Americans in their homes. They held him in high regard. He met with governors from New York and Virginia to discuss plans to improve trade among the colonies. William suggested they use a common currency and cooperate to fight crime. He urged politicians to "study peace and be at unity. Provide for the good of all."[30]

Back to England Again

William heard that the British legislature planned to turn all individually owned colonies into royal provinces, run by Parliament and the king. William knew he must go back to England to protect his colony. In November 1701, he and his family sailed for England. William and his family settled in a large home in Ruscombe. Sadly, William suffered several strokes. He wanted to return to Pennsylvania but was never able to do so. He died on July 30, 1718.

His family members retained the **proprietorship** of Pennsylvania, however, until the War of Independence, when it became one of the first 13 states. William's "holy experiment" was a success. Immigrants from all over Europe found a welcome home in Pennsylvania. The constitution William had helped to create provided for a system of **checks and balances** on governmental power. The ideals of liberty, justice, fairness, and tolerance served as an example for the U.S. Constitution and Bill of Rights. Thomas Jefferson called William Penn "the greatest lawgiver the world has produced."[31]

proprietorship: Right to own

checks and balances: A method to keep any one branch of government from having too much power

In Philadelphia today, there is a 37-foot statue of Pennsylvania's beloved founder, William Penn. It stands on top of city hall to honor this godly man, who for years stood watching over his city of brotherly love.

David Brainerd – Missionary to Native Americans

April 20, 1718 – October 9, 1747

Who Was David Brainerd?

David Brainerd was born in the little town of Haddam, Connecticut, in 1718. He was the sixth of nine children in the Brainerd family. His father was a wealthy and well-respected merchant. He also served on the governor's council in the state legislature. David had a happy, peaceful childhood. He loved fishing, swimming,  and ice skating in the winter months. He was home-educated by his parents. The children were taught languages, grammar, arithmetic, and most importantly, the teachings of the Bible. Their wise, loving parents faithfully taught them Christian doctrine and values that shaped their lives. Morning and evening, David's father led the family in devotions. They talked about the week's sermon they had heard in church or discussed certain passages of Scripture. Hymn singing was a daily practice. The principles David learned from the Bible would serve as a **compass** for his life's work.

Hardships Come

David's father died when he was just nine years old. The children helped their mother carry on in the years that followed. When David was 14 years old, his mother died, too. The care of the younger children was left to

compass: Direction

David's older sister. David tried his best to be a good farmer as his father had been, but it was a great challenge to him. He felt that he was created for something more than farming. He knew that God often leads us through the hard times, and that God helps us to grow through those experiences.

David worked on the farm during the daytime, but toward late afternoon, he hurried off to the Durham library. It had a large collection of religious and theological books. Reading was a great joy and privilege. David began to search his heart and he realized that although he knew much about God and the Bible, he did not have a personal relationship with the Lord Jesus. He knew verses and Bible stories but had never **repented** from his sin. He contemplated Romans 3:23 which says, "For all have sinned and come short of the glory of God." His sin began to bother him. He realized his

repented: Expressed sincere regret or remorse

deep need for a Savior. He read a book called *The Guide to Christ* that helped him. He repented of his sins and his attempts to gain favor with God by his good works. By God's grace, David was truly saved at the age of 21. That evening, with tears running down his face, he joyfully told God,

David Brainerd — Missionary to Native Americans

"I am so pleased and satisfied that you alone are God over all; that you alone are eternal and unchanging."[32]

Yale College

David immediately felt that God wanted him to dedicate his life to serving his Lord in full-time ministry. In 1739, he entered Yale College, which was established to prepare men for the ministry. At about this time, God was moving in a special way throughout the colonies. What was later called **The Great Awakening** was beginning to take place. God was using preachers to proclaim God's Word and thousands were repenting of their sins. God used men like George Whitefield to preach to crowds of people. He was an **evangelist** from England who traveled about the colonies drawing great crowds.

The Great Awakening: A time of spiritual awareness and revival

evangelist: Traveling preacher

Jonathan Edwards: Evangelist who did much to influence spiritual life in early America

When he preached, he had no microphones. He had a booming voice that carried well. One meeting drew 20,000 people. It was a unique time in the history of our country and many people, young and old, were repenting of sin and giving their lives to the Lord. David also heard **Jonathan Edwards** preach while in his first year at Yale. Many of the students at Yale were repenting of sin and becoming serious about serving the Lord. David became passionate about sharing the love of Christ with others. David would often see Native Americans around town. Many colonists seemed to look down on them, but David had compassion for them. They were human beings who needed Jesus Christ. They were excellent hunters, fishermen, and farmers. David admired their skills. David began to preach to Native American people who lived in New York and Connecticut. David seemed to be gifted to preach.

A New Mission

David deepened his time alone with God. Sometimes he spent an entire day in prayer. He would go to the woods alone, reading a small section of Scripture over and over again. He would pray over it and ask God to help him apply the truths in the Word to his own heart, mind,

and soul. He thought about and studied each word until he felt either blessed by it or convicted by it. Meditating on the Bible in this way became a daily habit and a deep source of strength and joy. On July 29, 1742, he stood before a representative from an association of ministers to be questioned for three hours regarding his knowledge of theology and how to communicate it to others. He passed the exam and was licensed to preach. He immediately had opportunities to preach, and people seemed moved by his words. One of the preachers who had invited him to speak accompanied him on horseback to preach to the Schaghticoke tribe. They were unsure if they would be welcomed or not. One of the braves spoke English and agreed to translate for them. David preached about the grace of God in the gospel of Jesus Christ. Native American men began to cry out for mercy and be distressed that they had no relationship with Jesus. God used David in a mighty way that day.

On the Road

On October 23, 1742, David set out on a 175-mile journey on horseback to preach from town to town. Over the next few months, he traveled over 1,200 miles preaching more than 60 sermons to men and women. "He wanted to wear himself out in service to the Lord."[33] Toward the end of the year, David was contacted by the Scottish Society, an organization created to carry out ministry and evangelism to the Native American people. He traveled to New York to meet with their board and was drilled again on his theology and what he would do in certain situations. When asked what he felt qualified to preach, David answered, "I believe that God, and no man, has qualified me to proclaim the excellencies of Christ, though I am nothing in and of myself."[34]

He was accepted and appointed to minister to the Native Americans in Kaunaumeek, New York. David arrived there on March 31, 1743. Life was hard among the tribe's people. David had an interpreter assigned to him, a Native American who went by the name of John. David at first stayed with a Scottish family, but soon built a little log cottage right in their village. From this location he had the opportunity to teach the people every morning and evening. He grew to call the Kaunaumeek "my people." He ate little food — mostly boiled corn and small loaves of bread. He slept on a pile of straw on top of a board. He requested permission to start a school among the Native Americans. They wanted to learn English to be able to better trade with the white men. David knew it would provide a great opportunity to teach them about the gospel.

With John's help, David began translating the Psalms into the Algonquian language. On Sundays, they would sing the words. He taught the basics of the gospel week after week. Then he taught an overview of the Bible, beginning in Genesis and working through the New Testament. John began teaching the children in the newly established school, and David often taught them, as well.

David was often afflicted with spells of sickness. He would feel weak and have bouts of sweating and fevers. Sometimes, he even coughed up blood. He realized that he was battling tuberculosis, the same disease from which his brother had died. However, he would not let it stop him in his mission. In times of sickness, he relied even more heavily on prayer to regain his strength.

David Brainerd — Missionary to Native Americans

Time to Move On

In the spring of 1744, David felt that God was tugging at his heart to move on to share the gospel with other tribes. His people begged him to stay, but David assured them there were other preachers nearby who could travel and preach. He felt he must go where tribes had no opportunity to hear the gospel. David traveled back to meet with the Scottish Society. He stopped to preach as he traveled, and also to rest when illness weakened him. He was offered two different preaching jobs at established churches along the way.

When he got to the Scottish Society, they wanted to send him to the tribes at the Forks of the Delaware River in Pennsylvania. He chose the hardest option. During the first week of March, he started on the journey through the wilderness alone. He had little food, no protection, and was constantly exposed to harsh weather. Many times along the way, he would cough up blood — a symptom of tuberculosis.

There were no doctors or medicine, but David trusted God to protect and care for him.

He arrived in May and met with local Native Americans, who welcomed him. A new interpreter joined him, Moses Tatamy, who was acquainted with Christianity but had not become a Christian.

Moses and David rode down to preach along the Delaware River. For two hours, David preached and appealed to the people to give up their idols and turn to the true and living God. The people began to cry out in conviction. David wrote in his journal, "Of late all my concern almost is for the conversion of the heathen; and for that end I long to live."[35]

The Native Americans were beginning to embrace Christianity. For the remainder of the summer of 1744, attendance grew from less than 20 to 50 people. David recognized that this was a work of God. He planted and watered, and God was giving the growth in people's hearts.

The Ministry Grows

On December 9, David and Moses Tatamy crossed the Delaware River and preached twice at Greenwich, New Jersey. While preaching this day, David became so moved that tears ran down his face. To his great delight, his interpreter, Moses began to weep. After the sermon, he explained to David, "I am in a miserable and perishing condition, David. I see plainly what I have been doing all my days, and I have never done one good thing. I have done many things folks call good

— I have been kind to my neighbors. But all of these things have not come from a heart of faith or of love of God. I want to turn and trust in Jesus to save my soul."[36]

From that day, David noticed a change in Moses' character and attitude. He was a new man! "Tatamy continued to interpret but now, not as a hired hand, but as a newborn believer. Tatamy felt compelled by the newfound joy and understanding of God's saving grace."[37] When David preached again with Moses at his side, he saw most of the people crying out for salvation. He was witnessing the fruit of his many labors among "his people." Throughout the winter, the people grew in their faith and desired to learn more of the depth of the riches of the gospel of Christ.

Revival

In 1745, David's journey led him to Crosswicks, a village in New Jersey. The people there had been suffering from a lack of food. While David was there, hunters killed several deer, and the people felt David's presence brought them blessings. This opened their hearts to hear his gospel message. People repented of their sins. They began to live differently. They stopped drinking alcohol and started treating one another with forgiveness. It was clear evidence they were being transformed by their newfound faith. Other Native Americans heard about the change in their lives and came to hear David preach. Revival was happening.

Converted, some Native Americans became evangelists themselves, carrying the message to other tribes. Each night, men would gather in David's tent to be discipled. They, in turn, would make more disciples. This was accomplished as David invested time and love in the lives of the men. One by one he was establishing deep bonds with them.

converted: Turning away from sin to Christ in faith

Last Days

David's body was becoming more and more racked with the effects of tuberculosis. He had high fevers, drenching sweats, and chills, and he coughed up blood. He was losing strength and losing weight. Eventually, he was forced to give up his missionary duties. His brother John stepped in to fill his place. David returned to New England. Before he left, the Native American community expressed their overflowing gratitude to the one who had suffered so much to bring them the life-giving message of Jesus. Tears flowed freely.

It was a terribly hard ride home for David because he was feeling so ill. He stopped to rest at the home of Jonathan Edwards, who **summoned** a doctor.

summoned: Called

David Brainerd — Missionary to Native Americans

The **prognosis** was bleak. Jonathan knew he must give David the news. David replied, "Mr. Edwards, I am willing and ready to be in heaven with my Lord. Countless times, I have desired this, but God has kept me here for a purpose — to make His wonderful gospel of Jesus known to the world. I am ready to die, whenever that day may come."[38]

prognosis: Likelihood of recovery

The daughter of Jonathan Edwards, Jerusha, offered to become his caregiver and tended to him in the Edwards home until he died. On October 9, 1747, 29-year-old David Brainerd passed from this life into the arms of his beloved Savior. Jonathan Edwards took David's journals, edited them, and had them published. The life of David Brainerd inspired countless missionaries, such as John Wesley, William Carey, and Jim Elliot. Thanks to Jonathan Edwards, Brainerd's life story has been read by millions and continues to inspire Christians around the world today.

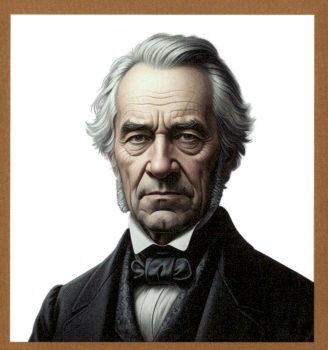

9

Noah Webster – Schoolmaster to America

October 16, 1758 – May 28, 1843

Who Was Noah Webster?

Noah Webster was born on October 16, 1758, near Hartford, Connecticut. He was one of five children. His father, also named Noah, was a farmer and a **weaver**. Mr. Webster served as a deacon in his church and as a justice of the peace in the community. Noah's mother, Mercy, was a descendant of William Bradford. Bradford had been the governor of Plymouth Colony established by the Pilgrims in 1620. Mercy taught the children to read and spell using the Bible. She also taught them to do arithmetic and play the flute. Noah enjoyed playing the flute. In his diary, he wrote that it amazed him how "the sound of a little hollow tube of wood should alleviate the heaviest cares of life."[39]

weaver: One who makes fabric

The children had to help with many daily chores on their 90-acre farm. Noah was diligent, but farm work was not interesting to him. He preferred to be reading and learning. After a hard day's work, the family enjoyed music and literature. Mr. and Mrs. Webster read to their children each night from the King James Bible. They recited stories and poems and sang psalms together.

Noah delighted in reading. He could think about words and their meanings for hours. Books were scarce. Noah read whatever he could get his hands on, including newspapers or even the yearly Almanac. He told his granddaughter years later that he would "take his Latin Grammar into the field and that his rests under the apple trees were quite too long for a farmer's son."[40] He was constantly full of questions. When troubles arose with England about unfair taxes, Noah was full of questions. His family would discuss issues at nighttime. His mother commented that Noah was different from her other children. He was a born "investigator."

Schooling

When he was 14 years old, Noah begged his father to allow him to study with a new minister who had come to Hartford, Reverend Nathan Perkins. He was a graduate of Yale College and knew Latin and Greek. Noah desperately wanted to learn the languages so he could read more books, since many were written in Latin. His father finally gave in, saying, "I wish to have you serve your generation and do good in the world and be useful."[41]

After studying for two years, Reverend Perkins recommended that Noah should attend Yale. His father **mortgaged** his house to pay for Noah's education. He traveled with Noah on horseback to take him to school. Noah found out that students had to get up at 5:30 each morning for prayers. Then they split wood, built fires for the school, and pumped water. After that, they had ten hours of instruction each day. Noah loved learning and excelled in it. The students took part in debates about current events, and as the war developed, there was much to discuss.

mortgaged: Borrowed money on

Wartime

Classes were interrupted at times during the War for Independence. When the war moved closer to the school, the students formed a student militia and conducted drills. They built barricades to protect New Haven, an important seaport town. Noah played the flute to help the students keep time when they marched. Once, General Washington stayed in New Haven on his way to Boston. The Yale students escorted him out of town. Noah led the way, playing Yankee Doodle on his flute.

Heroes of Early America

The war caused hard times for everyone. The college suffered as some students left to join the army. Some could no longer afford to attend school. Food was scarce at times so students were sent home. Classes had to be **suspended** at one time because of an outbreak of **typhoid fever**. In a nine-month period, classes were only in session for three months. Noah joined his father and brother in the Hartford militia briefly. Finally, in September 1778, Noah was able to graduate.

Noah graduated with excellent grades and gave the **oration** at graduation. When he returned home, his father told him that the war had ruined him financially. He was in danger of losing the farm he had mortgaged to put Noah through college. Noah was devastated. He determined he would find a way to repay his father and find a job as soon as possible.

suspended: Canceled temporarily

typhoid fever: A severe bacterial fever

oration: Speech

Noah Webster — School Teacher

Jobs were scarce during wartime. Noah decided he would teach school during the day. Evenings were spent reading law. His goal was to obtain a law license. He found a teaching position within a few days. Noah Webster won the respect of the children with his kindness. He was frustrated, however, by the lack of books and supplies. He had 50 children to instruct and only one spelling book. The Bible was the only book he had to teach reading. The building was cold and damp. The children often sat shivering with wet feet from having walked for miles in the snow to get there. The pay was not good. He told his mother one night, "There is so much wrong with our schools. I have been writing some essays on education. A new nation has been formed on the American continent, and our schools are backward and neglected. There must be some way to improve them."[42]

Noah determined that he would write a whole series of textbooks with everything the boys and girls of America needed to know. The following summer, he studied law under U.S. Supreme Court Justice Oliver Ellsworth. He taught himself French, German, Italian, and Spanish languages as well. He succeeded in attaining his law license in 1781.

American Books Needed

The war was over, but things were still strained in the colonies. People didn't have money to hire lawyers. The colonists had lost almost everything except their liberty. Noah made some money by writing essays for newspapers, mostly

about the condition of schools. He wanted to "engage children to be diligent and make them fond of books."[43] But the teachers' books that did exist were all about England. Children needed new books — American books by American writers. He wrote that children should learn in smaller-sized classes, "never more than 20 or 25 pupils under one instructor."[44] Comfortable desks and chairs of differing sizes were needed. Girls were to be educated as well as boys. Every citizen should be able to learn to read. He advocated for instruction for African Americans, even if they were adults.

America was a land of citizens who had immigrated from many different countries, so several distinct accents and **vocabularies** were blended into everyday speech. "Let us establish a national language as well as a national government," he suggested.[45] Noah believed Americans needed to develop their own spelling books. He wanted words to be spelled the way they were pronounced without using extra letters. He experimented with removing silent letters. That was never totally accepted, however.

vocabularies: Words

Noah Webster — Schoolmaster to America

Noah would stay up late at night to work on writing his series of textbooks. He titled his first book, *The American Instructor*. It was a simple speller, full of patriotism and words from the Bible. It was completed in January 1783. It contained 119 pages, full of history, geography, science, creation of the world,

character lessons, spelling of proper names, names of countries and states, rivers, towns, and counties. Noah included sections of the Declaration of Independence and excerpts from famous speeches. His spelling books broke words into syllables to help with pronunciation. He corrected **faulty** pronunciations. At that time in the country, people spelled words any way they saw fit. Noah Webster wanted to standardize spelling. In his books, he tried to make grammar fun. Noah knew that children loved and learned from rhymes. He made lists of words that sounded alike and made simple rhymes to help children remember. He made up rules for difficult pronunciations, for example,

faulty: Wrong

"The consonant c is hard like the k before a, o, u, l, and r, such as cat, but always soft like s before e, i, y, as cellar."[46]

Obstacles to Overcome

Noah Webster ran into obstacles when he tried to get his spellers into the hands of the public. First, there were no American publishers yet. Second, there were no copyright laws. These laws show who has the exclusive legal right to reproduce, publish, sell, or distribute something such as a literary, musical, or artistic work. And third, there were no bookstores. Not to be deterred, Noah worked to get copyright laws passed by going to state legislatures. He succeeded in getting six states to pass them. He contacted preachers and teachers, urging them to buy the American textbook. He approached newspaper offices and got an agreement from a printer to print 5,000 copies of the speller. The printer agreed to wait for his money. If the spellers didn't sell, Noah would be responsible to pay for them. He talked to owners of stores and drugstores, getting them to agree to try selling the spellers.

Slowly the books began to sell. Children loved the stories and fables, and so did adults. The 5,000 copies were sold in nine months and larger amounts were printed. In ten years, a million copies were sold. It soon became the **backbone** of American education.

backbone:
Foundation

By Noah Webster's death, 25,000,000 copies were sold. It had sold more copies than any book except the Bible. It became known as *The Blue-Backed Speller* because of its **distinctive** blue cover. The foundational principle of the *Blue-Backed Speller* was that "God's Word contained in the Bible has furnished all the necessary rules to direct our conduct."[47] Webster believed that the basis of American education in all subjects must rest upon Christianity. Over the years, Noah wrote American history books and geography books, as well as a biology text about animals.

> **distinctive:** Having an uncommon and appealing quality

Politics

Noah met Benjamin Franklin, who became a **mentor** to him. He began to study government. He wanted to influence our country's Constitution. Noah wrote a book called *Sketches of American Policy*. His book **advocated** a strong central government that protects its people and their property. George Washington and James Madison complimented him on the book and its ideas. James Madison quoted his book later at the Constitutional Convention. He wrote to Noah, crediting him with ideas that were adopted in the Constitution. Noah wrote essays and gave speeches urging states to adopt the Constitution. He sold his books when he traveled and made many friends. He was invited to many dinners around the country.

> **mentor:** Advisor
>
> **advocated:** Endorsed

During a visit to Philadelphia in 1787, he met Rebecca Greenleaf. They had much in common, and they were married in 1789. The couple moved to New Haven, Connecticut, and had the first of their eight children in 1790. Noah became involved in local politics. He was a member of the city council and later served as justice of the peace. He was elected to the state legislature as well. He greatly influenced the education system of New Haven. He served on the  school board and was elected its president; he organized and helped build a new school. Noah loved teaching his own children. He used his estate as a science classroom for them, teaching them about plants, animals, and weather. Entertaining his family with his flute playing and singing was one of his delights.

The Dictionary

America's first dictionaries were small, having relatively few words. They still used old British spellings. Noah studied dictionaries. In 1800, he began a six-year project to compile and define 40,600 words for *A Compendious Dictionary of the English Language*. It ended up being 408 pages. The following year, he published a school dictionary with 30,000 words in 312 pages. He determined to write an even larger dictionary.

Noah had to move his family to Amherst, Massachusetts, so he could farm to help support the family while he worked on his dictionary. As always, finances were tight, so for the next nine years, the family lived in Amherst. There, a need developed for a college to prepare young men for the ministry. Noah Webster  helped start one. His family was asked to provide music for their church. And the church had no Sunday school, so Noah set one up. By the summer of 1822, he had been working on his dictionary for 15 years. He estimated it would take another three years to complete. He moved his family back to New Haven to be closer to more libraries.

As he sought to define each word in his dictionary, Noah found that he needed to know its **origin** and how it had been used in previous years. He traveled to England and France with his son William to research dictionaries. When he entered the library in Paris, the sight of 800,000 books stunned him. After eight weeks in Paris, they left for Cambridge, England, to spend the winter at Cambridge University's library. He personally learned 28 languages so he could understand the original language from which any word was **derived**. He wrote to his wife, "At no time for forty years

origin: Where it began to be used

derived: Where its source was

past, have I been able to accomplish more business daily, that I have both in France and England."[48]

To illustrate the meaning of the words he was defining, Noah used each one in a sentence. A large percentage of the sentences he chose as examples were Bible verses. The dictionary was nearing completion. He later recalled, "I was sitting at my table in Cambridge, England, in January 1825. When I had come to the last word I was seized with a trembling which made it difficult to proceed. However, I summed up the strength to finish the last word, and then, walking about the room a few minutes, I recovered."[49] *Webster's 1828 American Dictionary of the English Language* was finished at last!

Noah and William sailed for home. Then Noah had to **edit** the manuscript and find a publisher willing to print it. In November 1828, about 2,500 copies came off the press, just after Noah's 70th birthday. Webster dedicated his dictionary to God in the preface.

Many people gave him the title, "The Father of the American Language." For his contributions to education, he earned the nickname of "Schoolmaster to America."

edit: Make final changes or corrections

Noah Webster — Schoolmaster to America

Noah Webster lived another 15 years. During that time, he wrote a *History of the United States*. He also authored a completely new translation of the Bible. He wrote six more books for use in schools. In May of 1843, Noah went to church as usual. He spent the entire day there because there was afternoon prayer and time to socialize. When he returned home he was shivering. By the end of the week, he had grown seriously worse. Weak from fever he whispered, "I'm ready to go. My work is all done. I know in whom I have believed. I have struggled with many difficulties. Some I have been able to overcome, and by some I have been overcome. I have made mistakes, but I love my country, and have labored for the youth of my country, and I trust no precept of mine has taught any dear youth to sin."[50] That evening Noah Webster died. President John Tyler said, "The nation has lost one of its most illustrious citizens. Noah Webster played a vital role in the initial formation of this government, the education of its youth, and the strength of the nation's fabric. America is in his debt."[51]

10

Peter Francisco – A One-Man Army

July 9, 1760 – January 16, 1831

Who Was Peter Francisco?

Historical evidence suggests that Pedro Francisco was born on July 9, 1760, on an island in the Azores off the coast of Portugal. From his earliest memory, he had lived in a mansion near the sea. He remembered playing in a beautiful garden with his sister. His mother spoke French and his father another language he did not understand. The family was entertaining guests one day. He and his sister were sent out to play in the garden. They were given cakes, toys, and candy, so they were happily playing. Suddenly some men broke through the bushes and grabbed both Pedro and his sister. His sister struggled and screamed and finally broke away. Pedro was blindfolded, tied up with ropes and chains, and carried aboard a ship. He remembered being on the ship for a long time. He never discovered why this happened. He never saw his family again.

City Point, Virginia

It was in the early morning hours of June 23, 1765, when James Durell, an eyewitness, reported, "A foreign ship sailed up the James River, dropped anchor opposite the dock, and lowered a longboat to the water with two sailors in it. Then a boy of about five years old was handed down and rowed to the wharf, where he was deposited and abandoned. The boat returned quickly to its ship. The ship weighed anchor at once, sailed back down the James River...."[52] Two farmers came over to ask the boy if he was okay. He did not answer. Finally, he spoke, but in Portuguese. All they could understand was Pedro Francisco. His clothes, though soiled from the long trip, showed that he was born to a family who was wealthy. His leather shoes were **adorned** with expensive silver buckles on which were the initials PF – Pedro Francisco.

> **adorned:** Decorated

People gathered around the boy. He was given food and then taken to Prince George County's poorhouse. His story soon spread through the surrounding counties. Judge Anthony Winston, Patrick Henry's uncle, lived in Buckingham County. He heard of the boy's **plight**. On his next trip to City Point, he visited the lad and decided to take him to live on his 3,600-acre plantation. He arranged for a tutor to teach English to Pedro (now called Peter). Judge Winston was very fond of the boy and when Peter learned enough English, the judge questioned him about his past. He told him the few memories he had. All of Peter's life, his past remained a mystery to him.

> **plight:** Unfortunate situation

Peter Francisco — A One-Man Army

Early Life

Peter grew up with Judge Winston. He was apprenticed as a blacksmith when he was old enough. By the time he was 15 years old, Peter stood six feet, six inches tall and weighed 260 pounds. He was a whole foot taller than most of the grown men in the area and incredibly strong.

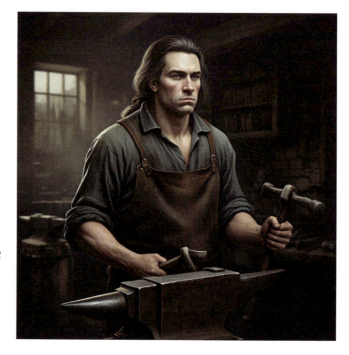

Judge Winston was a **staunch** Patriot. He knew trouble was brewing with England. Peter learned about the struggle for independence from the judge. Peter developed a **fierce** sense of patriotism. When Judge Winston attended the Second Continental Congress, Peter went with him. Here he met George Washington, Thomas Jefferson, Patrick Henry, and other important Patriots. He listened while Judge Winston's nephew, Patrick Henry, gave his **rousing** speech in St. John's Church. It was the famous "Give me liberty or give me death" speech. Peter left inspired. He wanted to do something to help. When Washington called for able-bodied men to join the army, Peter volunteered.

staunch: Dedicated

fierce: Very strong

rousing: Exciting, calling others to action

Time for War

Judge Winston had a uniform made especially for Peter due to his large size. Peter was a full 11 inches taller than the average soldier and very muscular. Peter was assigned to the Tenth Virginia Regiment. The Battle of Brandywine Creek was his first battle. He was 16 years old. That battle would have been disastrous for Washington's army except for the service provided by the Tenth Virginia. They were the rear guard and held the British at bay for a full 45 minutes, which gave Washington time to retreat safely. Peter fought admirably but was wounded in the leg by a musket ball. He was nursed by a Quaker family. In that home, he met the Marquis de Lafayette, who also had been wounded. While recovering, the two became fast friends.

More Action

Less than a month later, Peter was present at the Battle of

Germantown. Again, the American army faced defeat. During the retreat, Peter single-handedly carried many wounded men to safety. Then he was sent to guard Fort Mifflin, a fortification on an island in the middle of the Delaware River, close to Philadelphia. The attack on Fort Mifflin was one

Peter Francisco — A One-Man Army

the fiercest battles of the war. It was estimated that 1,000 cannonballs fell every 20 minutes. The log walls of the fort began to crumble. Peter's great strength was invaluable. He could round up and carry twice as many logs as the other soldiers. He could also build fortifications higher than anyone  else due to his height and long, strong arms. The siege left 250 of the 450 soldiers killed or wounded. Peter carried many of the dead and wounded to the mainland. He then set fire to the ruins, escaping to the Jersey shore. He spent the winter at Valley Forge with Washington's men. Peter's great strength was an asset in chopping down trees and building huts for all the men.

Under Anthony Wayne

Peter was chosen by General Washington and Baron von Steuben to be in an **elite** fighting regiment. He was injured again when a musket ball hit him high in the right thigh. It could not be removed and caused him pain for the rest of his life. Peter's fame was becoming well known throughout the Continental Army. George Washington **commissioned** a special sword to

elite: Specialized

commissioned: Specially ordered

be made for Peter. It was a five-foot **broadsword**. Peter was known for getting close up to the enemy and using his sword. He had actually broken one sword in battle, which is why Washington had one specially made for him.

> **broadsword:** A sword with a wide blade

Stony Point

The British were in control of the fort at Stony Point, New York. Washington decided to storm their defenses using the Corps of Light Infantry under the command of General Anthony Wayne. This was an elite group of the best men in the army from five different states. Peter was a member. He was chosen not only for being a good soldier, but also because he always boosted the **morale** of the soldiers.

The attack was to be in darkness to achieve complete surprise. Peter volunteered for the most dangerous duty. They had to cross a marsh to get to the fort. While other men sank in the mire, Peter's extra height and strength helped him not only to get across but to pull men along with him. As one of the axmen, he chopped savagely at the **abatis**, opening a gap in the defenses. Again and again, he swung his ax, opening up passages for the Patriots to enter the fort. Peter received his third wound — a slash to the abdomen. Before he lost consciousness from loss of blood, he killed two more British **grenadiers**, including the one who had wounded him.

> **morale:** Confidence

> **abatis:** A barricade made of sharpened branches

> **grenadiers:** A group of Britain's strongest soldiers

Peter Francisco — A One-Man Army

Of the 20 men who took on the dangerous mission, only three survived unharmed. Captain William Evans, who was present, wrote, "Francisco was the second man who entered the fort and distinguished himself in numerous acts of bravery and **intrepidly** ... in a charge which was ordered to be made around the **flagstaff**, he killed three British grenadiers and was the first man who laid hold of the flagstaff and being badly wounded laid on it that night and in the morning delivered it to Colonel Fleury. These circumstances brought Mr. Francisco into great notice and his name was **reiterated** throughout the whole army."[53] Peter was taken to Fishkill, New York, where he recovered for six weeks. He fought at the Battle of Paulus Hook in August, though still in pain. His first enlistment drew to a close, but Peter's resolve had not.

> **intrepidly:** Extremely daring
>
> **flagstaff:** Flagpole
>
> **reiterated:** Repeated

The Battle of Camden

When Peter learned that the British were turning their attention to the South, his loyalty to his state caused him to re-enlist. This time he joined Colonel William Mayo's Virginia Militia Regiment. Fighting with the militia was quite different from fighting with trained troops. Militia troops frequently were not well-supplied with equipment. When under heavy fire, many of the men ran from the battlefield.

Peter Francisco and a small number of **seasoned** soldiers tried to stop their retreat. A British grenadier was just about to bayonet Colonel Mayo when Peter rushed up and "put a ball and three buckshot" into the British soldier. Dragging him off his horse, he passed the horse to Colonel Mayo who was then able to ride off to join his men. Colonel Mayo never forgot this act of bravery on his behalf. After the war, Colonel Mayo presented Peter with a dress sword which is now on display at the Virginia Historical Society in Richmond.

seasoned: Experienced

When Peter tried to rejoin his men, he discovered that the horses that pulled the cannon had been killed. Not wanting to leave the cannon behind for the British, he unhitched the 1,100-pound weapon from its **gun carriage**, hoisted it to his shoulder, and carried it off to safety. After rescuing the cannon, he was exhausted and resting under a tree when one of British Lieutenant Colonel Banastre Tarleton's men came galloping up. "Surrender or die!" the **trooper** yelled. "My gun isn't even loaded," Peter calmly responded. He stood and held his musket horizontally to the ground which was known to be a gesture of surrender. As the cavalryman reached for the gun, Peter spun it rapidly and thrust his sword into the soldier.

gun carriage: Mount

trooper: Military private

Peter Francisco — A One-Man Army

Shortly after that, he was surrounded by more of Tarleton's men. He pretended to be happy and hollered, "Huzzah, my brave boys! We've conquered the rebels!" He tricked the British into thinking he was one of them and rode off to safety. He was not only strong but clear-headed in times of danger.

The Battle of Guilford Courthouse

Reports from Guilford Courthouse, North Carolina, said Peter Francisco killed 11 grenadiers single-handedly. He then had his leg pinned to his horse by a British bayonet. He managed to use the same bayonet to attack his **assailant**. Although injured badly he continued to fight until he was pierced again. The sword entered above his knee and was thrust all the way up to his hip. He desperately clung to his horse and rode a short

> **assailant:** The person who had attacked him

distance, then he fell to the ground. A kind Quaker woman found him later and took him home to nurse him to health. This time it took eight weeks for the awful wounds to heal. His heroism at Guilford Courthouse was soon **broadcast** throughout the Southern Army. As soon as Peter's wounds were healed up enough, he limped over 190 miles back home to Virginia, because he did not have his horse. General Nathanael Greene presented Peter with an engraved razor case as a tribute for his **valor**.

> **broadcast:** Proclaimed, heard

> **valor:** Bravery

Francisco's Fight

Once back in Virginia, Peter volunteered for active service. He became a scout, reporting on the movements of British Lieutenant Colonel Banastre Tarleton's army. Tarleton and his men had a reputation for undue **brutality**. In May 1780, Tarleton's men defeated a Patriot force. When the Americans attempted to surrender, 75% of them were killed or wounded.

One night Peter stopped to rest outside of Wards Tavern in Amelia County. Suddenly, nine of Tarleton's men rode up. Eight of the men went inside but one demanded that Peter give him his shiny silver shoe buckles. Peter told him to come get them if he wanted them. As he bent over to yank them off Peter's shoes, Peter suddenly grabbed the man's saber and defended himself with it. The other eight men came to see what was happening. One shot at Peter, but Peter was quicker with the saber. Another shot and the bullet grazed Peter's side but again, Peter was quick with the saber. Ben Ward, the tavern keeper, passed one of the **dragoons** a musket. The dragoon fired at Peter, but the gun misfired. Peter grabbed it from the man's hand and struck him with it. Then he jumped onto his horse and the rest of Tarleton's men fled on foot.

> **brutality:** Cruelty
>
> **dragoons:** British cavalrymen

Peter seized the tavern keeper who had almost cost him his life. Ben pleaded for mercy. Peter commanded him to hide the eight horses that were left behind in exchange for his life. Tarleton's men caught up with their colonel, reporting what had happened. Tarleton himself then pursued Peter, but Peter, knowing the countryside well, **eluded** capture. The next day, Peter went back to the tavern to retrieve the horses. He kept the best horse for himself and named him "Tarleton."

eluded: Avoided

He sold the other horses the next day and gave the money to the government. Tarleton became his favorite horse. He rode it for many years. The incident at the tavern became known as Francisco's Fight and earned him the name of "The Virginia Giant." A painting of the scene hangs in Independence Hall in Philadelphia. Peter had the satisfaction of being present at Yorktown to see the British surrender.

After the War

Lafayette and Peter remained friends. Peter's family told the story of how he met his future wife. He and Lafayette were walking in front of St. John's Church where Patrick Henry had given his famous speech. They saw a young woman trip, but before she could fall, Peter ran and caught her. She was Susannah Anderson, and they ended up getting married. The marriage took place in 1784 when Peter was 24 years old.

Peter was appointed Sergeant-at-Arms for the Virginia House of Delegates. He served in that position until his death in 1831. Historians think he died of appendicitis. The House of Delegates gave him a burial with the full honors of war, praising him for "his extraordinary strength, his **undaunted** courage, and his brilliant feats."[54] A monument in his honor in New Bedford, Massachusetts, recorded this tribute from George Washington: "Without him we would have lost two crucial

undaunted: Fearless

battles, perhaps the war, and with it our freedom. He was truly a one-man army."[55]

132   Heroes of Early America

Glossary

abandoned: Left alone.

abatis: A barricade made of sharpened branches.

adorned: Decorated.

advocated: Endorsed.

Anglican: Official church of England.

apprenticed: Sent him to learn a trade from a skilled workman.

Archduke Ferdinand: Ruler of Austria.

arduous: Hard, requiring considerable physical effort.

aristocracy: Nobility.

assailant: The person who had attacked him.

backbone: Foundation.

barricade: Temporary enclosure.

beckoned: Gestured to.

broadcast: Proclaimed, heard.

broadsword: A sword with a wide blade.

brutality: Cruelty.

bubonic plague: A serious, usually fatal, infection spread by fleas.

catapults: Launchers.

cavalry: Soldiers on horseback.

celebrity: Famous person.

checks and balances: A method to keep any one branch of government from having too much power.

confiscated: Seized.

consequently: As a result.

contemplated: Thought about.

converted: Turning away from sin to Christ in faith.

commissioned: Specially ordered.

compass: Direction.

critical: Important.

custody: Protective care.

derived: Where its source was.

detained: Seized.

directives: Orders.

disembarked: Left the ship.

distinctive: Having an uncommon and appealing quality.

dragoons: British cavalrymen.

duke: A male ruler in England.

earl: British nobleman.

edit: Make final changes or corrections.

egregious: Obviously bad.

elite: Specialized.

eluded: Avoided.

entourage: A group of people attending to the needs of an important person.

escort: Lead.

evangelist: Traveling preacher.

executed: Put to death.

expelled: Made to leave.

expired: Died.

exploits: Daring feats.
extinguished: Put out.
faulty: Wrong.
fierce: Very strong.
flagstaff: Flagpole.
flintlock: Gun fired from a spark.
fortified: Protected.
gawk at: To stare or observe.
The Great Awakening: A time of spiritual awareness and revival.
grenadiers: A group of Britain's strongest soldiers.
gun carriage: Mount.
heir: Person entitled to inherit property or rank.
hold: Place for storing cargo.
horrified: Greatly distressed.
immigrants: People who move to another country permanently.
immune: Having antibodies to avoid getting the disease.
interpreter: One who translates speech.
intrepidly: Extremely daring.
Jonathan Edwards: Evangelist who did much to influence spiritual life in early America.
joust: Contest with lances.
kidnap: Take someone away illegally.
Latin: The main language used by schools, churches, and the state in Europe.
leased: Rented.
liberation: Freeing them.
looting: Confiscating goods in a war.

Glossary

magistrate: Civilian judge.

marooned: Stranded.

menial: Lowly.

mentor: Advisor.

mercenaries: Hired professional soldiers.

merit: Advantage.

monastery: A building where monks live.

monks: Catholic religious men living under strict rules.

morale: Confidence.

mortgaged: Borrowed money on.

muskets: Light guns with long barrels.

opportune: Favorable.

oration: Speech.

origin: Where it began to be used.

Parliament: The ruling body of England.

parsonage: House and lands provided for a preacher.

Philadelphia: Meaning "the city of brotherly love."

plight: Unfortunate situation.

plundered: Took goods as an act of war.

pneumonia: A bacterial or viral lung infection.

pounds: British money.

pretense: False appearance.

privateers: Privately owned, armed vessels hired to attack enemy ships.

procure: Obtain.

prognosis: Likelihood of recovery.

proprietorship: Right to own.

providential: Fortunate, determined by God.
recant: Publicly withdraw his beliefs.
reformed: Improved.
reiterated: Repeated.
repented: Expressed sincere regret or remorse.
reprisal: Revenge.
rials: Unit of Spanish money.
rousing: Exciting, calling others to action.
Royalist: Those who support rule by a king.
seasoned: Experienced.
shallop: A light wooden boat used as a rowboat.
shunned: Avoided.
sighted: Seen.
smallpox: A contagious viral disease.
stability: Reliability.
staunch: Dedicated.
stipulation: Condition.
strategies: Plans to achieve military successes.
summoned: Called.
suit of armor: Protective clothing made of metal.
surreptitiously: Secretly.
suspended: Canceled temporarily.
tasked: Given the job.
thatched: Made from grasses.
theological: The study of God and His relationship to the world.
tracts: Pamphlets.

Glossary

traitors: Those who betray their country.

trooper: Military private.

tuberculosis: A serious illness affecting the lungs.

typhoid fever: A severe bacterial fever.

undaunted: Fearless.

valor: Bravery.

visor: Armor covering the face.

vocabularies: Words.

Wampanoag people: Native American tribe living in that area.

weaver: One who makes fabric.

Corresponding Curriculum

The *What a Character! Series* can be used alongside other Master Books curriculum for reading practice or to dive deeper into topics that are of special interest to students.

This book in the series features famous early heroes of America, whose stories would incorporate well for students in grades 6–8 accompanying history, language arts, vocabulary words and definitions, as well as geography studies and cultural insights. We have provided the list below to help match this book with related Master Books curriculum.

Chapter 1: Captain John Smith—Adventurer in the New World

America's Story Vol. 1	*Elementary U.S. Geography & Social Studies*
Children's Atlas of the U.S.A.	*Language Lessons for a Living Education*

Chapter 2: Myles Standish—Protector of the Pilgrims

America's Story Vol. 1	*World Geography and Cultures*
The World's Story	*Language Lessons for a Living Education*

Chapter 3: Squanto—Friend of the Pilgrims

America's Story Vol. 1	*World Geography and Cultures*
The World's Story	*Language Lessons for a Living Education*

Chapter 4: William Bradford—Father of the Pilgrims

America's Story Vol. 1	*World Geography and Cultures*
The World's Story	*Language Lessons for a Living Education*

Chapter 5: Pocahontas—Powhatan Princess

America's Story Vol. 1

Children's Atlas of the U.S.A.

Elementary U.S. Geography & Social Studies

Language Lessons for a Living Education

Chapter 6: John Alden—Pillar of Strength

America's Story Vol. 1

Children's Atlas of the U.S.A.

Elementary U.S. Geography & Social Studies

Language Lessons for a Living Education

Chapter 7: William Penn—Defender of Religious Freedom

America's Story Vol. 1

Children's Atlas of the U.S.A.

Elementary U.S. Geography & Social Studies

Language Lessons for a Living Education

Chapter 8: David Brainerd—Missionary to Native Americans

America's Story Vol. 1

Children's Atlas of the U.S.A.

Elementary U.S. Geography & Social Studies

Language Lessons for a Living Education

Chapter 9: Noah Webster—Schoolmaster to America

America's Story Vol. 1

Children's Atlas of the U.S.A.

Elementary U.S. Geography & Social Studies

Language Lessons for a Living Education

Chapter 10: Peter Francisco—A One-Man Army

America's Story Vol. 1

The Fight For Freedom

Elementary U.S. Geography & Social Studies

Language Lessons for a Living Education

America's Struggle to Become a Nation

Endnotes

1. Julianna Brennan Rodgers, *Captain John Smith: American Hero* (CreateSpace Independent Publishing Platform, September 4, 2017), 63.
2. Janet and Geoff Benge, *Captain John Smith: A Foothold in the New World* (Lynnwood, WA: Emerald Books, 2006), 135.
3. Ibid., 136.
4. Daniel K. Davis, *Miles Standish* (New York: Chelsea House Publishers, 2011), 14.
5. Ibid., 103.
6. http://mayflowerhistory.com/tisquantum.
7. William Bradford, *Of Plymouth Plantation* (New York: Alfred Knopf, 1952), 94.
8. Arthur Schlesinger, Jr., *William Bradford: Governor of Plymouth Colony* (Philadelphia, PA: Chelsea House Publishers, 2000) 46.
9. A.M. Anderson, *Squanto and the Pilgrims* (Chicago, IL: Wheeler Publishing Company, 1949), 125.
10. Ibid., 129.
11. Ibid., 154.
12. Gary Schmidt, *William Bradford: Plymouth's Faithful Pilgrim* (Grand Rapids, MI: Eerdmans Publishing, 1999), 6.
13. Arthur Schlesinger, Jr., *William Bradford: Governor of Plymouth Colony* (Philadelphia, PA: Chelsea House Publishers, 2000), 46.
14. Schmidt, *William Bradford: Plymouth's Faithful Pilgrim*, 94.
15. Ibid., 186.
16. John Smith, *The Generall Historie of Virginia, New-England, and the Summer Isles: with the Names of the Adventurers, Planters, and Governours from their First Beginning An 1584 to This Present 1626* (London: I.D. and I.H., 1632), 122.
17. Ibid., 122.
18. Victoria Garrett Jones, *Pocahontas: A Life in Two Worlds* (New York: Sterling, 2010), 95.
19. Ibid., 104.
20. Ibid., 109.
21. Ibid., 112.
22. Cecile Pepin Edwards, *John Alden: Steadfast Pilgrim* (Boston, MA: Houghton Mifflin, 1965), 50.
23. Ibid., 154.
24. Ibid., 155.
25. Janet and Geoff Benge, *William Penn: Liberty and Justice for All* (Lynwood, WA: Emerald Books, 1958), 32.
26. Ibid., 33.
27. Marty Rhodes Figley, *Who Was William Penn?* (Minneapolis, MI: Lerner Publications, 2012), 15.
28. Ibid., 17.
29. Ibid., 28–29.
30. Ibid., 36.
31. Benge, *William Penn: Liberty and Justice for All,* 196.
32. Brian H. Cosby, *David Brainerd: A Love for the Lost* (Scotland, U.K.: Christian Focus Publications, 2011), 20.
33. Ibid., 55.
34. Ibid., 59.
35. Ibid., 92.
36. Ibid., 101.
37. A.J. Lavanderos, *Who Is Missionary David Brainerd?* (Synergy Solutions, 2024), 35.
38. Cosby, *David Brainerd: A Love for the Lost,* 133.
39. Catherine Reef, *Noah Webster: Man of Many Words* (Boston, MA: Clarion Books, 2015), 6.
40. Pegi Deitz Shea, *Noah Webster: Weaver of Words* (Honesdale, PA: Calkins Creek, 2009), 4.
41. Ibid., 8.
42. Isabel Proudfit, *Noah Webster: Father of the Dictionary* (South Bend, IN: Bradford Press, 1942), 92.

43. Shea, *Noah Webster: Weaver of Words,* 17.

44. Ibid., 17.

45. Ibid., 17.

46. Ibid., 21.

47. Noah Webster, *The American Spelling Book* (Boston, MA: Thomas and Andrews, 1806), 156.

48. Shea, *Noah Webster: Weaver of Words,* 34.

49. Proudfit, *Noah Webster: Father of the Dictionary,* 200–201.

50. David Collins, *Noah Webster: Master of Words* (Milford, MI: Mott Media, 1989), 142.

51. Ibid., 143.

52. Sherry and Bobby Norfolk, *The Virginia Giant: The True Story of Peter Francisco* (Charleston, SC: The History Press, 2014), 16.

53. Ibid., 85.

54. Ibid., 132.

55. Ibid., 15.

Inspire Students with Biographies of **Notable Lives** from **HISTORY**.

Where Faith Grows!

America's War Heroes
Inventors and Scientists
Extraordinary Animal Heroes
Heroes of the War of Independence
Famous Women in History

Famous Pioneers and Frontiersmen
Amazing American Presidents
America's Famous Spies
Famous American Statesmen
Heroes of Early America